UP

– LEFT, RIGHT, UP, DOWN –
NEW DIRECTIONS IN SIGNAGE
AND WAYFINDING

LEFT

RIGHT

– LEFT, RIGHT, UP, DOWN –
NEW DIRECTIONS IN SIGNAGE
AND WAYFINDING

gestalten

DOWN

ICI LÀ

by FULGURO | Yves Fidalgo + Cédric Decroux
Designer – FULGURO
Client – Hors séries, Lausanne

741.
6
LEF

Mobile signal device that can be used outdoors as well as indoors. The foot also adapts to rough ground. This project was part of a collective exhibition conceived by INOUT, a group of 12 young Swiss designers.

Material ± Production – Thermolacquered steel
Photographer – © Yann Gross and Emilie Muller

"MY ENVIRONMENTAL
DESIGN IS MERELY AN
EXTENSION OF MY
GRAPHIC DESIGN IN
THREE DIMENSIONS AND
IN PUBLIC SPACE."

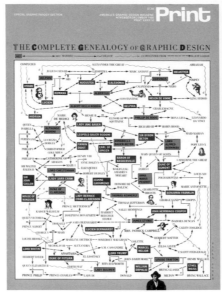

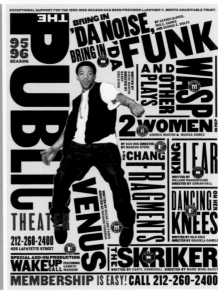

"The Complete Genealogy of Graphic Design" for *Print Magazine*, 1985. Designed by Paula Scher/Pentagram

1995-96 season campaign poster for *The Public Theater*, 1995. Designed by Paula Scher/Pentagram

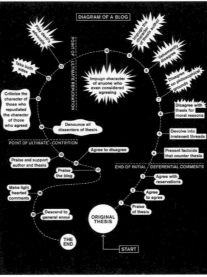

Environmental graphics for "The New 42nd Street Studios," 2000.
Designed by Paula Scher, Rion Byrd, Dok Chon, Bob Stern, Tina Chang/Pentagram
Photographer – Peter Mauss/Esto

"Diagram of a Blog" for the *New York Times*, 2007.
Designed by Paula Scher/Pentagram

Environmental graphics for "Achievement First Endeavor Middle School," 2010.
Designed by Paula Scher, Andrew Freeman/Pentagram
Photographer – Peter Mauss/Esto

– INTERVIEW –
WITH PAULA SCHER
PENTAGRAM, NEW YORK

Paula Scher studied at the Tyler School of Art in Philadelphia and began her graphic design career as a record cover art director at both Atlantic and CBS Records in the 1970s. In 1984 she co-founded Koppel & Scher, and in 1991 she joined Pentagram as a partner.

Drawing from what Tom Wolfe has called the "big closet" of art and design history, classic and pop iconography, literature, music, and film, Scher creates images that speak to contemporary audiences with emotional impact and appeal. Three decades into her career, these images have come to be visually identified with the cultural life of New York City.

Knowing your work and what your trajectory has been so far, it comes as a surprise that you also do signage systems. How did you come in contact with this area of design?

The advantage of being a partner of Pentagram is that sometimes you get the opportunity to work on projects that are totally new experiences. Clients believe in the expertise of Pentagram. Also, we have the resources and staff to back up the promise. When I worked on my first signage project you could say that I was really unqualified for the job. I didn't know how to read an architectural plan. I didn't understand some of the technicalities in the conversation.

Do you remember what your reaction was when you had to do your first signage system? Coming from a different creative field, which was your approach?

When I worked on "The New 42nd Street Studios," I had the advantage of approaching the design of the wayfinding from a graphic design point of view. I was interested in the navigational aspect of it, but also in the spirit of the place. It was a rehearsal studio for actors and actresses who take their cues from markings on the floor. I used the floor for wayfinding. It was much more effective that way.

Who commissions a signage system for a building? Is it the architect or the clients of the architect?

Both. Sometimes an architect hires us directly. Usually, if the client hires us it is because we had already designed the identity for the client and the signage becomes another part of the identity system.

At what stage are you being contacted? Is the building already finished or is it just planned?

We are hired at all stages. Sometimes we are hired when the building is still in a conceptional stage because it is important to get our input early on if the signage is going to be electronic or if it requires special lighting or other electrical needs. (This can be some four to six years before the building opens). The electrical wiring has to be installed in the appropriate places and electrical wiring is early in the building planning process. Sometimes signage is considered as an inexpensive add-on and we can be hired when the building is nearly complete (six months before the building opens). I've found it best to be hired either very early in the process or very late. It's good to be hired early. As I said, because you can have not only an effect on the wiring, but you may add something to the design of the flow of the space. It's good to be hired late because you have a clear understanding of what the parameters are and you tend to solve the problem quickly and effectively within those parameters. It's bad to be hired in the middle (two or three years before the building opens). You get neither benefit. You can't change any structure or infrastructure and you don't have the gratification of completing the job quickly. Generally you are mired in a lot of bureaucratic minutia and you end up making something not terribly interesting.

What is the line-up of your team when you do a signage system? How do you work together?

I have a graphic designer on my team (my associate Drew Freeman) who has learned the appropriate design programs for realizing design in three dimensions, virtual reality programs, as well as basic photo retouch, and illustration programs. He can also animate and do some programming. He works well with ar-

chitects, understands plans, knows how to review shop drawings, etc. I am totally dependent on him. We collaborate on all environmental projects and he also works on some graphic projects.

What is your approach today? After developing that many signage systems you must have adopted a methodology you work with.

Usually, I look at drawings or models. I usually can't walk through the space if it isn't built yet. The most important thing for me is to understand the use and spirit of a place.

I approach environmental graphics the way I approach an identity assignment. I ask these questions: How are people supposed to perceive the space? What feeling should they get from it? How can they intuit their way through it? What other information needs to be provided? Is there a narrative?

I answer these question in an initial concept presentation, which usually demonstrates several key areas like an entrance way or lobby, some major room signs, some directional signs, some back of house signs. The presentation demonstrates typography, color, material, messaging, and ultimately spirit. Then there are usually revisions as a result of the dialog among the architect and client. One thing I have found out is that when an environmental design is approved, it always comes out just like the approved photo-rendering, even if four years have elapsed since that rendering was initiated. In my graphic design projects, the work is often much more drastically altered from the initial comp to the finished piece.

The building itself constitutes an influential element of the project. On the other hand, the visual identity of the organization, institutions, or company that commissioned the signage system, also plays an important role. How do these influences mix?

Sometimes the sign system is based on the identity, especially if I designed the identity. Other times it is totally different, usually because the organization views the identity as something transitory and is interested in having the environment graphics conform to the specific architecture.

A signage system helps you find your way in buildings. What else is or what could be the task of a signage system? Or what could be the task of a signage system?

The point of all signage systems is to help a user gain an understanding of a place and a space. The systems can be purely functional, or motivational, or entertaining, or sometimes all of those things at once.

Long before you did you first signage system you made illustration that guided the viewer through your world. Where do you see the parallels between your signage work and your illustration/graphic design works?

My environmental design is merely an extension of my graphic design in three dimensions and in public space.

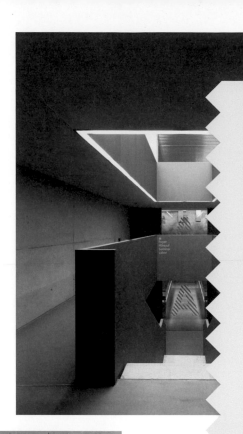

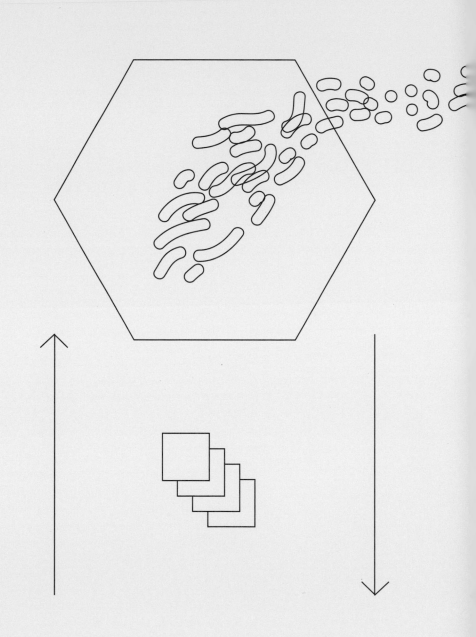

CHAPTER ONE
- TREATING SURFACE -

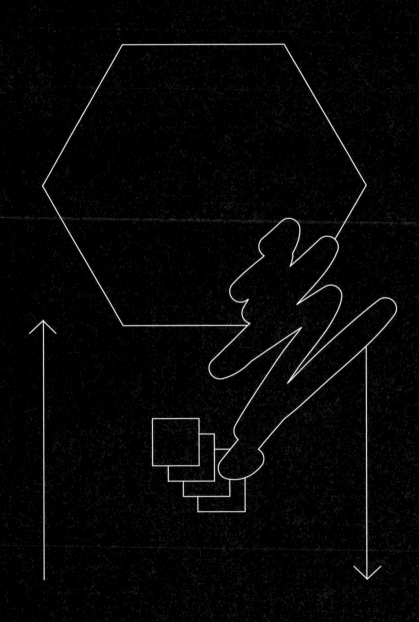

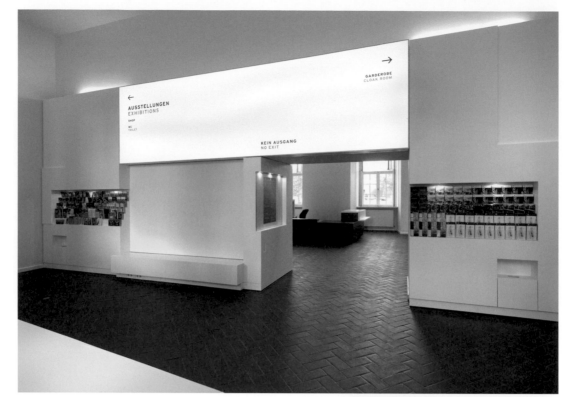

JEWISH MUSEUM BERLIN

by Polyform
Designer – Polyform, Büro für Grafik- und Produktdesign
Client – Jewish Museum Berlin

The target for Polyform was to create a system which in its appearance reacts to the deconstructionistic-expressive architectural idiom and integrates in an unobtrusive way. Compact ashlars were selected as information carriers that rest directly on the wall. They consist of solid-colored black plastic. The jointless connection to the wall and the dark individual color of the structures create the impression of abstract volumes protruding from the wall. The components of the system include floor plans, elements for orientation and signage elements, function plates, door plates, as well as elements for temporary information. In further expansion stages, the system was supplemented by other elements individually matched to the architecture, wall typography as well as large-scale information and routing in the lobby in the form of foil displays with background illumination. The system was awarded the Red Dot Best of the Best.

Typeface – Interstate
Material ± Production – Corian, translucent film
Architect – Daniel Libeskind
Interior design – Bromsky Architekten
Photographer – Stephan Klonk, Jens Ziehe

KUNSTMUSEUM DIESELKRAFTWERK COTTBUS

by SV Associates Ständige Vertretung Design and Communication GmbH
Designer – Nick Kapica
Client – Stadtverwaltung Cottbus

An expressionist diesel-electric power station designed by Werner Issel and constructed in 1927 was transformed into a contemporary art museum by Anderhalten Architekten. The wayfinding system has been designed to work with the powerful architecture: it provides a reference to the past while supporting the contemporary use. The typeface *Neo Futura* by Milton Glaser was chosen for all signs because its industrial feel provides reference to the original power station signs. Painted directly onto the concrete walls and applied as vinyl lettering to painted surfaces, it provides the museum with a simple and cost effective system. External signs are enamel bases with vinyl lettering applied. *Neo Futura* was also used for the advertising banner and flags creating an overall identity for the building.

Typeface – Neo Futura
Material ± Production – Vinyl lettering
Architects – Anderhalten Architekten
Photographer – Ursula Böhmer

BABYLON - MYTH AND TRUTH
EXHIBITION GRAPHICS AND SIGNAGE SYSTEM

by Polyform
Designer – Polyform, Büro für Grafik- und Produktdesign
Client – Staatliche Museen zu Berlin

In 2008, the Staatliche Museen zu Berlin presented, with this large exhibition in the Pergamonmuseum, the legends surrounding Babel and the truth about the ancient Babylon—two worlds in one exhibition. Based on the campaign developed by Meta Design, Polyform developed the staging of the outdoor area—banner surfaces on the building, large-scale projection of the temporary pavilion with ticket sales, cloakroom, and shop area as well as the visitor routing to both parts of the exhibition, and the entire exhibition graphic design—including room titles, quotations, ascending wall texts, and object lettering.

Typeface - QType, Absara
Material ± Production - Direct lettering

MUSEUM OF MODERN ART FRANKFURT, MAIN HALL EXHIBITION SIGNAGE

by Hauser Lacour
Designer – Stefan Hauser, Margaret Warzecha
Client – MMK, Museum of Modern Art Frankfurt

Corresponding to the artist's concept, the signage was purely typographic.

Typeface – Super Grotesk Reg, BP Romain Black
Material ± Production – Foil plott
Photographer – Axel Schneider

Playfully combined with the main exhibit signage in the central hall of the museum.

Museum logo on concrete wall, entrance area.

SURREALE WELTEN
CORPORATE DESIGN, SIGNAGE
SYSTEM AND FIRST INTERIOR, PLUS
MERCHANDISING AND CATALOGUE

by Gute Gestaltung
Designer – Gute Gestaltung
**Client – Staatliche Museen zu Berlin and Bundesamt für Bauwesen
und Raumordnung**

The Collection Scharf-Gerstenberg opened in 2008. It is located in the so-called Eastern Stueler building and in the Marstall (stables wing) opposite the Museum Berggruen and the Charlottenburg Palace. Paintings, sculptures, and works on paper by surrealists and their forerunners were shown on three floors under the title "Surreal Worlds." One typeface, *ITC Century*, is used throughout the corporate design. Its beauty and legibility work well as big logo-print on the wall of the entrance hall and as object signage. We used simple colors—orange, white, grey, black—and few materials.

Typeface – ITC Century
Material ± Production – Silkscreen print

Flags with adaption of Museum logo, outside; fabric.

Palindrome, exhibition area; silkscreen print.

Main display, entrance area; plotter foil.

Object signage, exhibition area; brass, card board.

Exhibition "Speed Limits," 2009. View of the installation at the CCA. © CCA, Montréal

Exhibition "Speed Limits," 2009. View of the installation at the CCA. © CCA, Montréal

Photography by Project Projects.

SPEED LIMITS

by Project Projects
Designer – Project Projects
Client – Canadian Centre for Architecture

"Speed Limits," an exhibition curated by Jeffrey Schnapp, examined the pivotal role played by speed in art, architecture, urbanism, graphics, economics, and modern life. Focused particularly on material cultures of the industrial and information eras, the exhibition marked the centenary of the foundation of the Italian Futurist movement. The installation at the Canadian Centre for Architecture was designed by Michael Maltzan Architecture with exhibition graphics by Project Projects.

Above the moldings in each of the show's seven galleries, large-scale historical quotations on the show's themes were set in *Luigi*, a typeface designed by Project Projects specifically for this exhibition. *Luigi* was inspired by the cover of Luigi Russolo's 1916 *L'Arte dei Rumori* (*The Art of Noises*), a Futurist manifesto stating the need for new music responding to intensified levels of noise in urban, industrialized daily life. The limited set of oddly shaped characters on Russolo's manifesto formed the basis for a full digital alphabet.

Typeface – Luigi (custom typeface), Bau

P#16

ACTIONS
WHAT YOU CAN DO WITH THE CITY

by Project Projects
Designer – Project Projects
Client – Canadian Centre for Architecture

"Actions," an exhibition at the Canadian Centre for Architecture in Montreal, explores how everyday human efforts can instigate positive change in contemporary cities. Activities such as gardening, recycling, playing, and walking are pushed beyond their usual definition by the 99 international architects, artists, and collectives featured in the exhibition. These experimental interactions with the urban environment show the potential for new forms of participation by city residents. Project Projects collaborated with the CCA on the exhibition design, which includes a large number of print pieces intended to provide a material form for documentation of ephemeral urban activities.

Typeface – History, Times New Roman
Photographer – Michel Legendre

BERLIN–NEW YORK DIALOGUES
BUILDING IN CONTEXT

by Project Projects
Designer – Project Projects
Client – Center for Architecture, New York

Project Projects was commissioned to design this exhibition for the Center for Architecture, New York and the Deutsches Architektur Zentrum, Berlin. The exhibition investigates three neighborhoods per city through complex sets of text, photographs, and data. Large-scale site and aerial photography create a sense of immersion in the urban contexts of each city.

Typeface – Fedra Sans, Greta

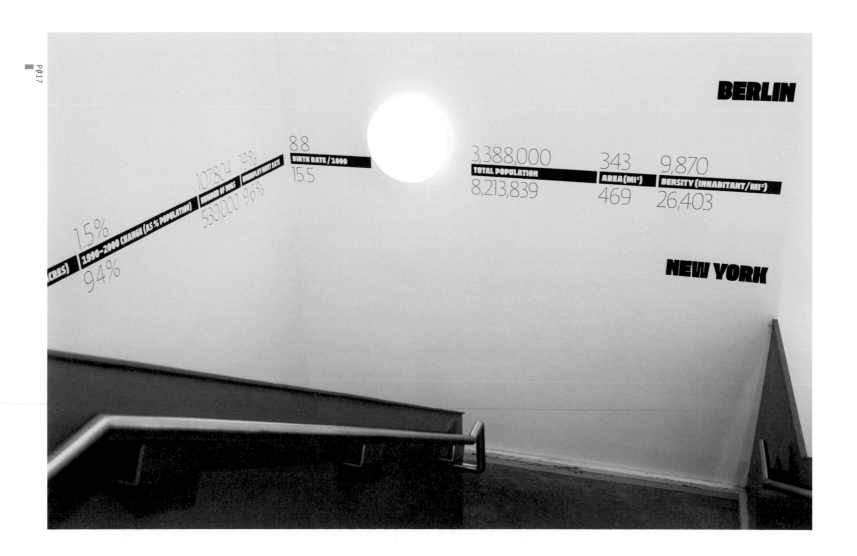

Signage for the forum area which consists of the two buildings, CCIB and Forum.

The signage systems that were created for temporary exhibition spaces not only guide the visitor, they also create an identity for the exhibition, within the identity of the exhibition space. What does this imply to the design?

There are various elements that should be taken into account:

1. The identity of the institution as well as the signage should have sufficient "personality," so that they can be differentiated from the exhibitions. They should co-exist but at the same time be easily distinguished.

2. The signage should not invade the exhibition spaces. Inside the exhibition space there should only exist "the exhibition" and its own signage (explanatory texts, titles, graphics, signs etc.).

3. To achieve a signage system that is sufficiently flexible to allow its adaptation to the exhibitions. This can be accomplished by the use of different media.

Mario Eskenazi

ABCDEFGHIJKLMNÑOP
QRSTUVWXYZabcçdef
ghijklmnñopqrstuvwx
yz1234567890.:;&@/()
[]{}¿?¡!←→+-_-

FORUM BARCELONA

by Mario Eskenazi
Designer – Mario Eskenazi, Ricardo Alavedra
**Client – Infraestructures del Llevant,
Ajuntament de Barcelona**

The "Forum Barcelona" is constituted by two different buildings. One by architect Josep Lluis Mateo and the other by Herzog & de Meuron. For the signage of the two buildings Mario Eskenazi and Ricardo Alavedra designed a bespoke typography, which was applied by taking into account the particularities of each building.

Typeface – Font Forum (bespoke typography)

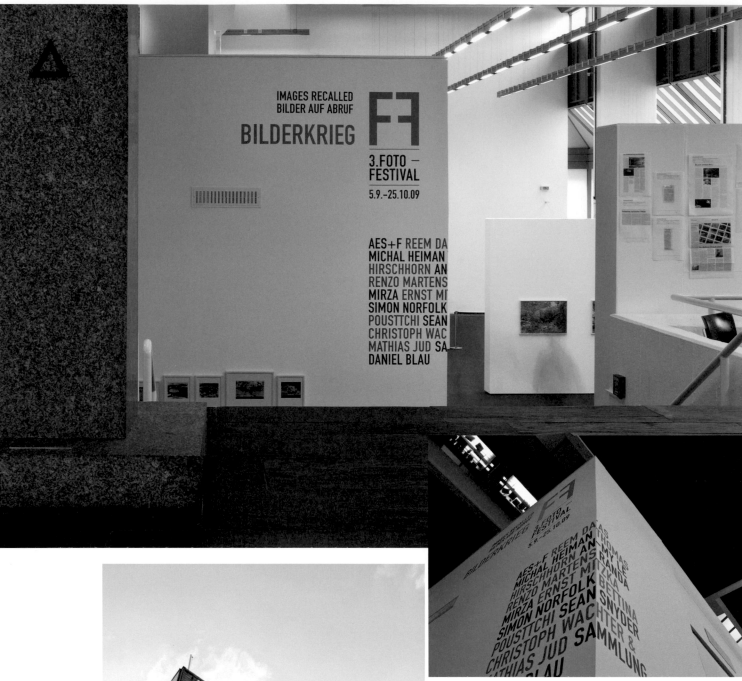

The name of the artists were placed with adhesive letters in the different sections of the exhibition in combination with the logotype.

Large outdoor print on the frontside of the Wilhelm Hack Museum in Ludwigshafen.
Photographer – Bettina Pousttchi, Parachutes 12, 2006 (detail)

Citylight poster and the outdoor exhibition in Mannheim. Panels with the descriptions of the artists

P#21

3RD FOTOFESTIVAL

by RAUM MANNHEIM
Designer – Frank Hoffmann
Client – Das Bildforum e.V.

The "3rd Fotofestival Mannheim Heidelberg Ludwigshafen"
in 2009 was the biggest curated photofestival in Germany.
The title of the year 2009 was "Images Recalled." The festival
presented the work of 60 international artists in six different
museums. RAUM MANNHEIM designed the logotype, differents
posters, panels, postcards, flyers, tickets, the website, and the
signage for the different exhibitions.

Typeface – DIN
*Material ± Production – Citylight, backlight foil, adhesive letters,
digital print*

UNIVERSITY OF APPLIED SCIENCE, WILDAU

by SV Associates Ständige Vertretung Design and Communication GmbH
Designer – Nick Kapica
Client – Brandenburgische Landesbetriebe für Bauen und Liegenschaften

A former train shed had been converted into a technical university building in Berlin. Wayfinding was required to identify the two new buildings within the existing shell. The specially adapted cross-hatched version of *Foundry Sterling Demi* reminds visitors of the former hazard warnings that could be seen on the trains and machines. *Medium* and *Book* were used throughout for door numbers, names, and directional information.

Typeface – Foundry Sterling
Material ± Production – Vinyl lettering
Architects – Anderhalten Architekten
Photographer – Ursula Böhmer

ORDNUNGSAMT FRANKFURT AM MAIN WAYFINDING AND ORIENTATION SYSTEM

by unit-design
Designer – Bernd Hilpert, Peter Eckart, Robert Cristinetti, Sabrina Flegel, Bruno Scheffler, Heidrun Althen, Margit Steidl
Client – OFB Projektentwicklung GmbH and Ordnungsamt Stadt Frankfurt am Main

The *Ordnungsamt* is valid alongside city hall as a representation of the city of Frankfurt and as an interface for the citizens. Comprehensibility, legibility, openness, and transparency of the services supplied are very important for this connection. In the dialogue with staff members and the head of the office, a solution was developed for the orientation system, founded on the greatest possible clarity and overview, while also responding to the specific character of the building's architecture from Meixner Schlüter Wendt. Thereby, the accentuated handling of typography, signs, and color played an important role. To achieve comprehensibility as high as possible for all user groups, service offers and instructions are represented by a system of easily recognizable signs and symbols.

Typeface – Thesis Sans
Material ± Production – Stencil print, foil cut, back printed glass for light boxes
Architects – Claudia Meixner & Florian Schlüter, Meixner Schlüter Wendt Architekten
Photographer – Eibe Sönnecken

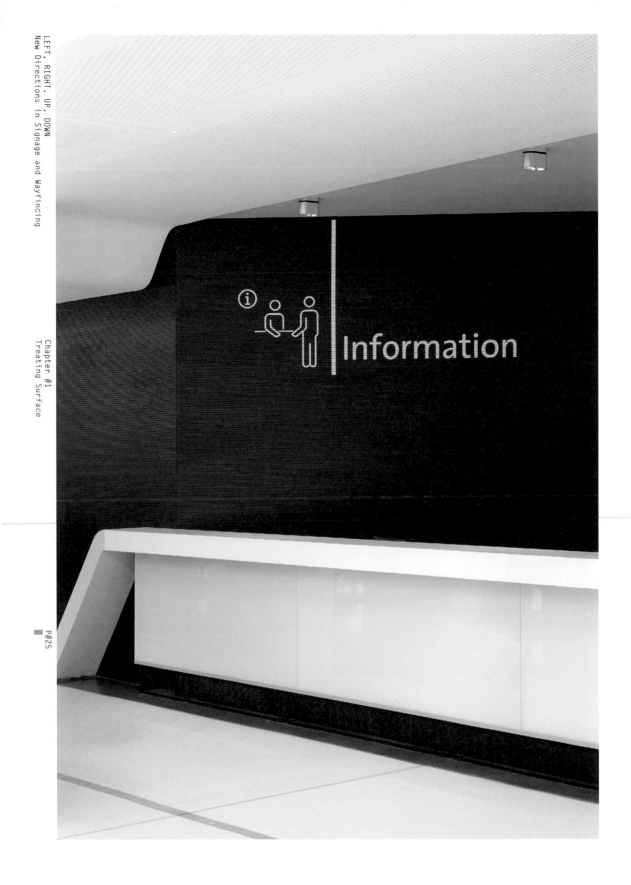

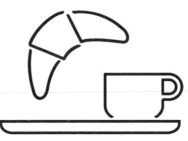

What do you consider an essential task for a signage system for workspaces?

A signage system can also be interpreted as a sign in a place that represents an "immediate transition." Alongside the content and form, this idea of transition may be an interesting tool for the design of a signage system.

When considering signage systems within workspaces, it is relevant to identify with the specific jobs or tasks of that workspace—apart from considering content-relevant aspects such as guidance and reflecting corporate identity. This component can be picked up as an idea of the signage system and be implemented through the design concept. Examples are: coins in a bank, moving letters or characters in the case of a sports company or a cell pattern, in a pharmaceutical company.

It is important to emphasize that the signage system has to be seen as a bridge between architecture and utilization. The custom-made development of these two components that belong together brings about a self-contained signage system concept.

Susanne Fritsch
Leitfaden-Design

HEADQUARTERS OF THE BANK
VOLKSBANK KARLSRUHE, GERMANY

by Leitfaden Design
Designer – Leitfaden Design
Client – Herrmann + Bosch Architekten

Task

The new headquarters building of the Volksbank in Karlsruhe, planned by the architects Herrmann + Bosch Architekten, required a suitable signage system with expandable functions, such as blinds and wall designs.

Architecture

The architects describe their project as "3xL"; a building that is partitioned by three atrium sections. 3xL stands for light, air, and quality of life. These qualities are complemented by an ecological approach. This is how the outside of the building looks like, facing the street; a "protective shield" facade is penetrated by three vertical and asymmetrical cut halos—the so-called "open spaces" indoors. Moreover, they play a main role in the orientation of the building: they are the unifying element of the floors, both visually and functionally (through stairs and elevators). The rear side of the building is partly glazed and faces a park. The interior space comprises open office levels with noise insulation and glass walls. The main entrance of the building is located on the narrow side of the building. Two side entrances are integrated into the protective shield facade. The entrance to the underground garage is also located in this part of the building. This administration building is primarily used by internal staff. There is also a customer area on the ground floor that has a reception area and rooms used for customers, seminars, and training.

Design concept and appliance

The essence of the idea is a gilded theme: "Bubbly coins of gold, silver and copper." This represents a substantive connection with the bank and blends well into the existing "light-air" concept of the architecture and its color and shape design. Furthermore, it also breaks up co-existing rigid structures such as large wall areas and glass surfaces. The concept for color is unfolded by the three atrium sections; as previously mentioned, they represent the entrance and connection between the levels. Thus the orientation system of each atrium features either gold, silver, or copper coins. Special typographical applications such as room names or important room numbers have a vertical font (made of dots). All the other typographical applications, such as labels on mailboxes and indicators for exit, entrance, delivery, and others, were set in a sans serif font that matches the overall design concept. An easy-to-understand pictorial language, contained within the coins, has been developed and applied to sub-labels such as toilets, cloakroom, cafeteria, and lockers. The entrance to the seminar and training rooms are located on a 26-meter-wall. To label these entrances, the bubbly coins (dots) were placed broadly on the wall together with a dot-font number, resulting in a overall picture. These coins were also used as a design element in the interior of the seminar rooms. The transparent architecture resulting from the glass facade and glass partitions had to be modified in some special cases: in archive rooms, the medical room, as half screens in conference rooms, and as walking protection. For this purpose the concept was used in its inverted form—that is to say, the coins were punched out from the foil. In the foyer, the logo of the bank was rasterized with silver dots and applied on a backlit screen of approximately 7 x 4 meters, thus creating a connection with the existing corporate identity of the bank. All the design elements were fabricated with adhesive foil, which was then adjusted to fit different surfaces and backgrounds.

Typeface – Atomic Clock Radio, DIN
Material ± Production – Adhesive foil
Location – Ludwig-Erhard-Allee 1, 76131 Karlsruhe, Germany
Architects – Herrmann + Bosch Architekten
Floor space – approx. 7,400 sqm

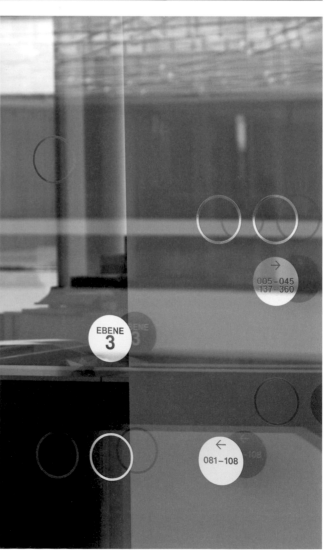

NEW BUILDING
DRÄGERWERK AG & CO. KG AA

by büro uebele visuelle kommunikation
Designer – Katrin Dittmann, Andreas Uebele
Project manager – Rebecca Benz, Katrin Theile
**Client – Molvina Vermietungsgesellschaft mbH & Co. Objekt
Finkenstraße KG**

The building is a glazed structure that twists and turns, ribbon-like, around courtyards and pathways. All the external walls and internal walls that face the atrium are glazed. This transparency makes it easy for visitors to identify where they are in reference to the interior and exterior of the building. Graphic symbols cover the internal glass walls, helping to define the different moods of the various locations. The wayfinding system consists of a base motif that is modulated in six variations. At its core is a simple, grid-style pattern of rings that is different on each story. The spacing of the rings varies in two directions, creating gaps, clusters, and distinctive formations. The information is incorporated within the pattern by filling in rings to create surfaces. The codes for different rooms, levels, and sections of the building are displayed within these circles. The pattern shapes are non-directional and non-prescriptive: they have their own equilibrium, and can be extended at will in any direction. They overlay the glazed walls like a transparent net curtain or a shimmering breeze, varying the look of the facades and also helping to prevent people from walking into the glass. The material used in the design has an incorporeal quality: the architecture and its environment are mirrored in the highly reflective film, appearing as a light, mobile, and shimmering image in the slender rings and circle shapes. Visually the circle is a strong shape: self-delimiting, self-referential. A circle has no straight lines to connect it with other edges or lines. Dealing with this geometrically interesting form becomes challenging when other, non-circular elements come into play. Text within a circle cannot be set in the normal way: flush-left is easy to read, but in a circle it produces odd shapes around the text. A clear margin becomes apparent only when several lines can be seen together, which is the exception rather than the rule. Individual words, meanwhile, look positively odd when set in this way: depending on their length, they may appear to be centered—but in fact the spaces to left and right are marginally different, in a way that's difficult for the eye to measure, creating a troubled effect. When arrows or symbols are added, the effect is even less attractive because these graphic elements unbalance the surface area. The system responds to this problem with an unconventional typographic solution: in line with the circle's rigorous visual rules, the type is aligned with a central axis that relates to the symmetry of the ring. The use of block capitals evens out the marginal spaces, calming the overall visual effect.

Typeface – Dräger Sans
Architects – Götz und Hootz Architekten BDA
Photographer – Michael Heinrich

BASEL LAND STATE ARCHIVES, LIESTAL

by Bringolf Irion Vögeli GmbH, Visuelle Gestaltung
Designer — Natalie Bringolf, Kristin Irion, Judith Stutz
Client — Hochbauamt Kanton Basel-Landschaft

The public area of the state archives is on the 2nd floor of the
building, at the same height as the railroad embankment nearby.
The font *Folded* was specifically developed for the building
and applied directly to the window surfaces on reflective foil.
Visitors and guests of the archives can see the typeface from two
perspectives: from a distance it indicates and labels the building,
at close range the letters are perceived as an ornamental banner.

Typeface – Folded (Bivgrafik)
Material ± Production - Screen print on glass
Architects – EM2N Architekten, Zurich
Photographer – Hannes Henz, Zurich

BERARDO COLLECTION MUSEUM SIGNAGE SYSTEM

by R2 Design
Designer – Lizá Ramalho, Artur Rebelo
Client – Berardo Collection Museum

Signage system for the Berardo Collection Museum—a modern and contemporary art museum located in Lisbon, Portugal. The entrance had a large empty white wall—the visitors' first point of contact with the museum. R2 Design aimed to forge a dialogue between visitors and the museum. They used text balloons to tell them what they could or couldn't do inside the museum. The wall thus became a plastic device. The floor number signs were designed from the details of each floor layout. The bathroom signs resembled standard male and female symbols, but when viewed close up, formed a wide array of male and female figures—tall and short, thin and fat, children and adults.

Material ± Production – Vinyl
Photographer – Fernando Guerra

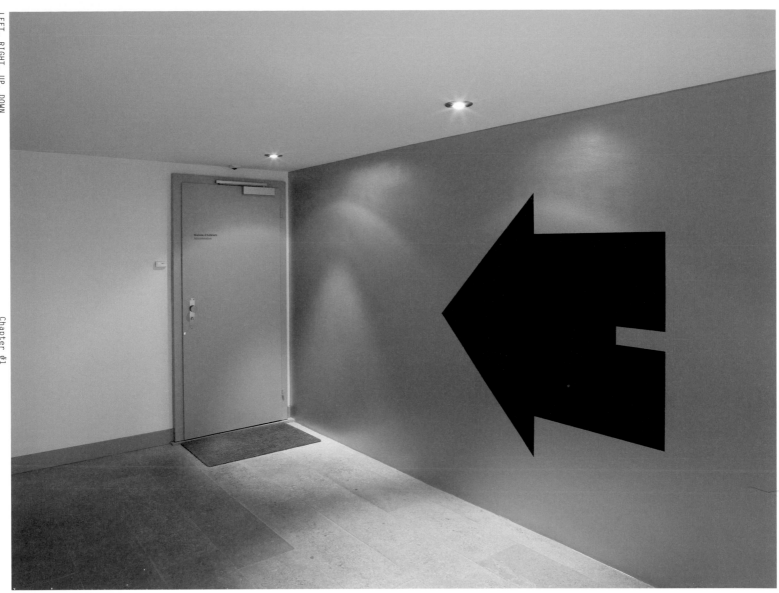

MAISON D'AILLEURS

by Notter + Vigne
Designer – Notter + Vigne
Client – Maison d'Ailleurs

Signage system for Maison d'Ailleurs (House of Elsewhere), a museum of science fiction, utopia, and extraordinary journeys in Yverdon-les-Bains, Switzerland. The logo that we designed for the museum represents both a house and an arrow. We used it here to indicate the entrance of the museum's administration offices.

Material ± Production – Wall stencils
Photographer – Mathieu Bernard-Reymond

SCHWEIZER FERNSEHEN STUDIOS 11-13
(SWISS TELEVISION STUDIOS 11-13)

by Büro4
Designer – Büro4
Client – Schweizer Fernsehen, Zurich

Signage and wayfinding system for the news studios 11, 12, and 13 of Swiss Television (SF), Zurich. Specific information and big numbers help visitors to easily find the way to the correct studio—even in cases of high tension.

Typeface – Neue Helvetica LT
Material ± Production – Acrylic paint on wall
Art direction – Cordula Gieriet (SF Gestaltung)

TAKEO TOKYO BAY DISTRIBUTION CENTER

by Hiromura Design Office
Designer – Masaaki Hiromura
Client – TAKEO Co., Ltd.

The signage system is for the logistic center of the TAKEO general trading company, built in the Tokyo Bay District. Simple and bold signs rather than decorative ones were intended as the main objective for this center's handling of products.

Photographer – Nacása & Partners Inc.

301/315

Drama & Dance Studios
Changing Rooms
Lecture Theatre Control Room
Production Studio
Music IT & Edit Studio
Classrooms
Seminar Room
Lift, Stairs & Toilets

61 individually painted directional wall signs throughout the college building at main junctions and decision making points. Signs consisted of large room numbers and smaller departmental headings and facilities.

Typeface – Customized DIN
Material ± Production – Black emulsion paint on white painted plasterboard walls

Facilities and directional graphics painted directly onto wall surfaces, including painted plasterboard, concrete brick, and concrete slab.

Material ± Production – Paint on concrete block

NORTH GLASGOW COLLEGE

by Marque Creative
Designer – Rhona Findlay, Hector Pottie, Marcel Bear
Client – North Glasgow College

045/056

Workshops
The Hub
First Aid
Toilets
Exit to Staff Car Park
←

Floor levels and directional super-graphics painted directly onto wall surfaces, including painted plasterboard, concrete brick and concrete slab.

Material ± Production – Paint onto concrete slab

Facilities and directional super-graphics painted directly onto wall surfaces, including painted plasterboard, concrete brick, and concrete slab.

Material ± Production – Paint on concrete slab

800 mm x 1500 mm, galvanized steel monolith for external landscape wayfinding.

Typeface – Customized DIN, stencil version
Material ± Production – 10 mm galvanized steel

Front elevation sign above main entrance, constructed from aluminum, each letter 700 mm tall, weighing approximately 8 kg. Developed in consultation with RMJM Architects to complement the building's facade and not interfere with the building's strong architectural statement.

Typeface – Customized DIN
Material ± Production – Suspended aluminum letters
Production and installation – Endpoint Ltd.

Welcome to North Glasgow College   Welcome to North Glasgow College   Welcome to North Glasgow College

8 meters long LED corner wrapping sign, positioned in the main reception, set flush within oak feature wall adjacent to main staircase.

Material ± Production – Integrated LED sign

Vitreous enamel map with eight spot colors fitted to custom-made oak bench. Bench was specially made to complement existing concrete benches used in the exterior landscaping. Map is a unique artwork and the bench sits in the main foyer, adjacent to the reception desk.

Typeface – Customized DIN
Material ± Production – Vitreous enamel, oak
Production and installation – Endpoint Ltd and Fairlie Furniture Works

DESIGNERS FAIR

by RADAU – Gestaltung!
Designer – RADAU
**Client – Büro Sabine Voggenreiter &
Heimatdesign**

The Designers Fair is a trade show in
Cologne, Germany that takes place at
the same time as the imm cologne. It
is a reasonable way for young interior
designers to show their work. RADAU
created a new guidance system covering
two floors of the Rheintriadem for the
Designers Fair in 2009. It consisted
of large geometrical forms made of
transparent black and pink foils, which
lead visitors from one room to the next.
Those forms, resembling giant splinters of
glass, were not only for guidance but also
for decoration of the building. Each room
was decorated with smaller circles cut out
of paper, which held all the information
about the exhibitors and their work.

*Typeface – Neutraliser Alternative Regular
Material ± Production – Black and pink PVC
foil, film plots on chipboard*

SCHILLERSCHULE AALEN

by Sven Völker
Designer – Sven Völker, Nils Völker
Client – Schillerschule Aalen

Typeface – Arial

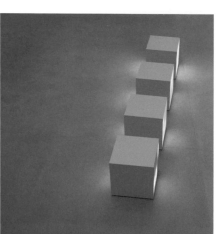

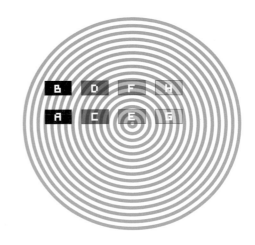

MTZ, MÜNCHNER TECHNOLOGIE-ZENTRUM

by L2M3 Kommunikationsdesign GmbH
Designer – Frank Geiger, Sascha Lobe
Client – Stadtwerke München

The signage system for the Münchner Technologiezentrum combines media elements with graphical, analogue elements to create a unified whole. Starting out from an assumed center point in the entrance area, concentric circles stretch out around the building. An information wall in the entrance area shows the visitor where the building the company he is looking for is located, and introduces him to the color coding system. The illuminated cubes point the way to the appropriate part of the building with the aid of animated typography. The colors stand for the various building modules. Visitors also find concentric circles on the ceilings in the staircase cores. The varying curve of the circles defines the distance from the center. In addition, there is a touchscreen intercom system in the entrance area. With just a few presses, you can get to the company and also view the building as a whole.

Typeface – MTZ
Architects – h4a Randecker & Gessert Architekten
Photographer – Florian Hammerich

SHINONOME CANAL COURT CODAN

by Hiromura Design Office
Designer – Masaaki Hiromura
Client – Urban Renaissance Agency

The large estate development project in Shinonome, Tokyo, is divided into six districts.
The common terraces and corridors are partially striped with a color specified to each
floor. Residents can easily identify their own buildings with the color and pattern specific
to each building.

Architects – Riken Yamamoto (Block 1)
Photographer – Nacása & Partners Inc.

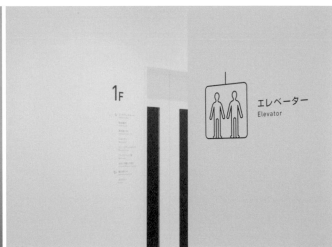

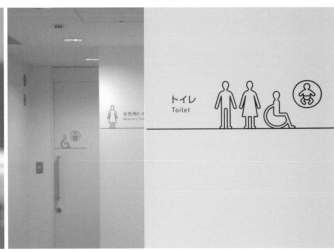

YOKOSUKA MUSEUM OF ART

by Hiromura Design Office
Designer – Masaaki Hiromura
Client – Yokosuka City

A museum located in Yokosuka, which faces the sea. Pictograms of a silhouette of a person are used to guide visitors around the museum. Preference is given to visitor-friendly signs over functional signs.

Photographer – Yasuo Kondo

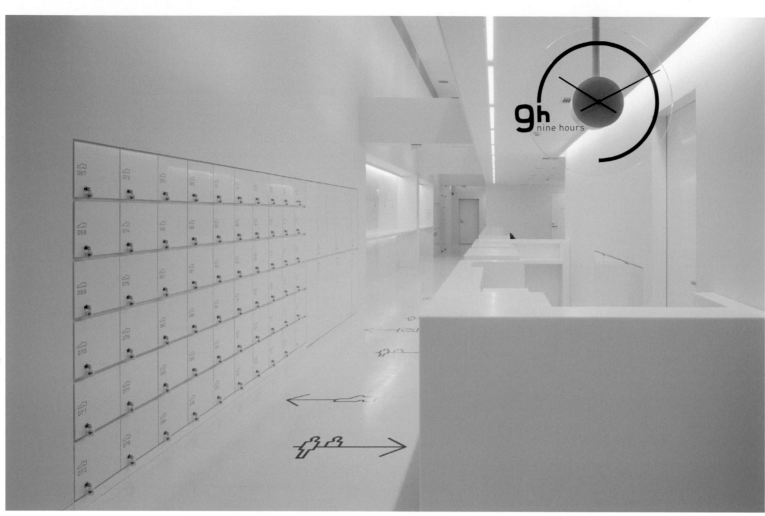

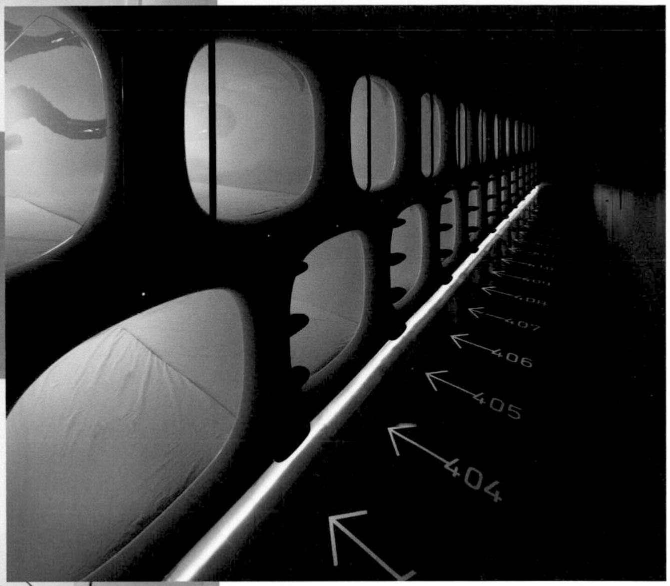

9H NINE HOURS

by Hiromura Design Office
Designer – Masaaki Hiromura
Client – Cubic Co., Ltd.

"9h Nine Hours" is an original type of a stay called "transit capsule," based on the idea of 1h (shower) + 7h (sleep) + 1h (dressing). 9h, where people stay in a capsule unit, was created to become an infrastructure in urban limited space and it suggests a new style of a stay with its original design. Graphic, interior, and product designers shared the concept and ideas from the beginning of the plan and every single piece of the facility was designed from the ground up. In terms of the signage system, the pictograms on the wall and the floor explain how to use the facilities, which is easy for foreigners to understand as well.

Creative director – Fumie Shibata
Interior – Takaaki Nakamura
Photographer – Nacása & Partners Inc.

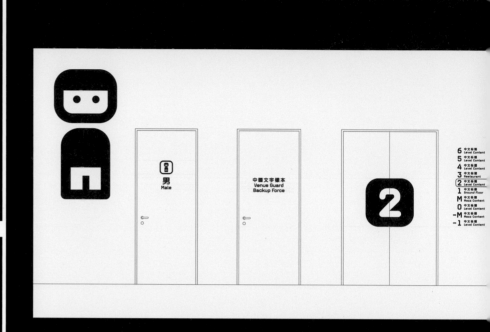

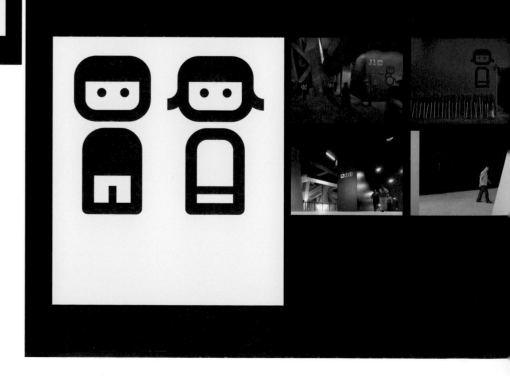

NATIONAL STADIUM BEIJING

by New Identity
Designer — New Identity
Client – Herzog & de Meuron

For the National Stadium Beijing, an orientation and signage system had to be developed that would safely and properly guide the 91,000 spectators to their seats within the filigree architecture designed by Herzog & de Meuron. The 12 sectors, easily recognizable from a distance, channel the large audience. The signage displays communicate the various elements such as numerals, typography, and pictograms in a consistently plain, graphic style, harmonizing English and Chinese typographics as well. The peculiarity of the system is its information transfer, which is exclusively restricted to the architectural girders as well as walls and columns; it completely dispenses with any form of free-standing signposts, columns, or panels.

Photographer – Iwan Baan, Amsterdam

Wayfinding is finding the way: in a functional, targeted and efficient manner. Can you find your seat or not?! Can you find the exit or not?! Yes or no—and if it's anything in between, you're lost! This applies always and everywhere in public spaces, but in particular to theaters and stadiums. Whether quickly dispersing large crowds of people, or getting 92,000 spectators into a stadium before kick-off—and afterwards quickly and safely out again: every gate and every exit that can't be found can become a problem.

Wayfinding must be functional, and it can also look good! Functionality becomes form, form becomes content, and the sign communicates the message! Simple and contemporary graphic design instead of redundant or complex presentation of information—it is self-explanatory, self-evident. Design perceives a location as a brand, translating architecture and interpreting it.

Bön Bannholzer
New Identity Ltd.

LIMOGES ZENITH (CONCERT HALL)
SIGNAGE SYSTEM

by Benoît Santiard
Designer – Benoît Santiard
Client – BTuA Bernard Tschumi urbanistes Architectes

Signage for a concert hall, in collaboration with BTuA (Bernard Tschumi urbanistes Architectes). This project was the starting point for designing a specific typeface, *Capitale*, along with pictograms. The straightforward design of this condensed font is intended to fit with the raw selection of materials used for the building, and maximize space for written informations.

Typeface – Capitale
Material ± Production – Painting, cut-out self adhesive vinyl letters
Architects – BTuA Bernard Tschumi urbanistes Architectes
Photographer – Julien Attard

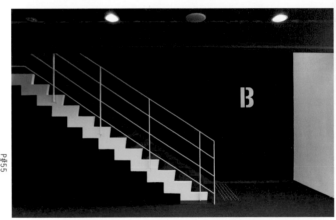

SENZOKU GAKUEN COLLEGE OF MUSIC

by TERADADESIGN ARCHITECTS
Designer – Naoki TERADA + TERADADESIGN ARCHITECTS
Client – Senzoku Gakuen College of Music

TERADADESIGN was responsible for providing the interior color design and signage design for Black Hall, a newly opened school (2009) for rock and pop music. Inside the school are recording studios, lesson rooms, and practice rooms, all sealed with no windows in order to provide a controlled musical environment. It was assumed that maintaining creative motivation in such environment would not be easy. The designers attempted to solve this problem with a strategic use of color. Various color combinations were adopted to serve different needs. All designed elements link to the total signage system.

Architect – Nihon Sekkei

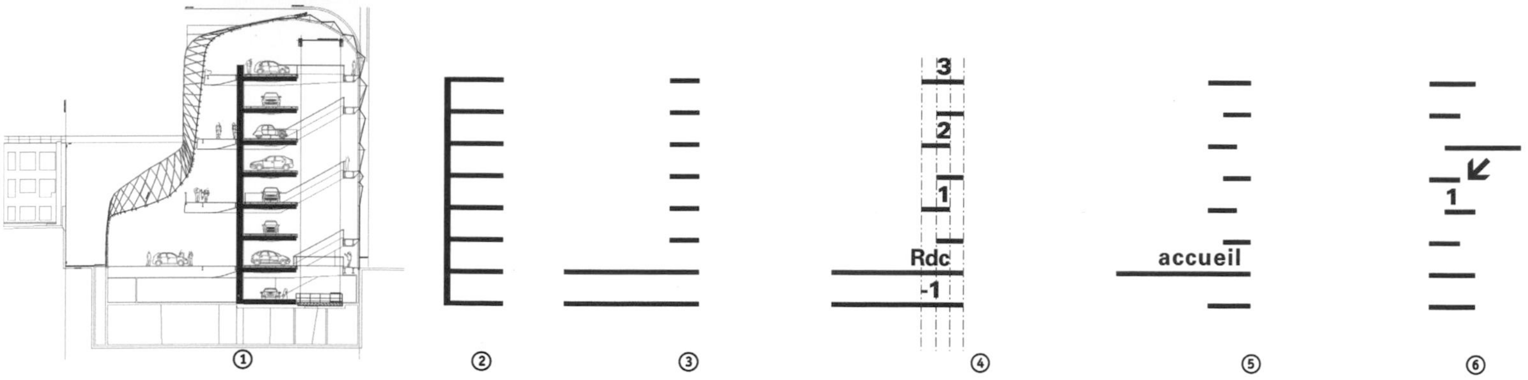

① bâtiment

② colonne vertébrale

③ Tournettes seules

④ + texte en Univers 65 Bold
chiffres en Univers 75 Black

⑤ identification

⑥ orientation

CITROËN SHOWROOM

by Nicolas Vrignaud
Designer – Nicolas Vrignaud
Client – Citroën

The design is an abstract pattern, an ideogram of the organization of the space. It is based on the structuring element of the building: car displays that create sequences in the vertical space.

Typeface – Univers
Material ± Production – Silkscreen print

PENSEÉ SAUVAGE

by Hauser Lacour
Designer – Laurent Lacour, Sven Michel
Client – Frankfurter Kunstverein

The main exhibit signage for "Penseé Sauvage" was integrated
into the exhibition.

Typeface – Knockout 70, Georgia
Material ± Production – Wall drawing
Photographer – Jonas Leihener

GROUND FLOOR MACBA

by Hauser Lacour
Designer – Laurent Lacour, Sven Michel
Client – Frankfurter Kunstverein

Ground floor signage for the exhibition of the collection of the
Museu d'Art Contemporani de Barcelona.

Typeface – Knockout 70, Sign Painter
Material ± Production – Wall drawing

GROUND FLOOR PENSEÉ SAUVAGE

by Hauser Lacour
Designer — Laurent Lacour, Sven Michel
Client — Frankfurter Kunstverein

Ground floor signage for the exhibition of Gardar Eide Einarsson.
The new exhibition information was added up on the prior.

Typeface – Knockout 70, Georgia, Sign Painter
Material ± Production – Wall drawing

01 **02**

CHAN-
TIER
TÉLÉGIL.

- MARION
- DEGIEZ
- GURTNER
- GÉRARD
- DOMINGUES
- VALLON

07/02/2005: Début chantier

19 **20**

TRIPOD
GÉRARD (CH)
DIT: *LEON*
48 ANS
CARRELEUR
PATRON

«C'EST UN MÉTIER CRÉATIF.
«CELA DEMANDE BEAUCOUP
«D'ARMONIE ET UN ŒIL.»
H

3/02/2005· Début carrelage

03 **04**

UN MAGASIN
FERME. IL EST
BIENTÔT REM-
PLACÉ PAR
UN AUTRE.
UN ESPACE DE
TRANSITION
ABRITE ALORS
LES TRAVAUX
DES LOCAUX
À VENIR.

CETTE VITRINE
ÉVOLUTIVE
EST DÉDIÉE AUX
ACTEURS DE CET
ENDROIT ET À
LEUR RÔLE DE
PASSEUR SANS
QUI RIEN NE
SE FERAIT.

21 **22**

DOMINGES
SERGIO (P)
DIT: *POMMADE*
38 ANS
CARRELEUR
EMPLOYÉ

«ET UNE FOIS QU'ON ARRIVE Y'A
«PLUS BESOIN DE BRANCHER LA
«RADIO, ON EST LÀ»

09 **10**

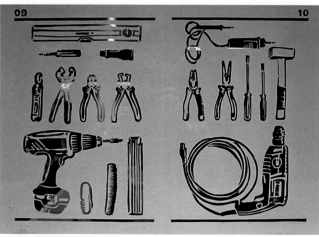

27 **28**

VALLON
MICHEL (CH)
54 ANS
DIT: −
ÉBÉNISTE
INDÉPENDANT

«MON CONCURRENT DIRECT C'EST
«LA BAGNOLE ET LES VACANCES »

07/03/2005 Début meubles

26

ÉRÈSE
JI RIT
«QUAND
«ON LA
«BAISE»[1]

«PE-
«QUENO
«COM-
«BOIO»[1]

[1] POMMADE
04/03 2005: Fin electricité (2)

[1] POMMADE
04/03/2005. Fin carrelage

CHANTIER TÉLÉGIL

by Régis Tosetti
Designer — Régis Tosetti/ECAL

"A shop closes down. It is replaced soon by another. A space of transition takes place in between. This evolutionary window is dedicated to the workers without whom nothing would happen and to their role of *passeur*." The passer-by was invited to follow the evolution of their work, day after day. The communication mixes the typology of newspapers and white painting, a common way to mask refurbishment work.

Typeface – Akzidenz Grotesk
Material ± Production – Water-based painting
Window – 280×200 cm
Dedicated to Gilbert & Monique

BIKEWAY - BELÉM-CAIS DO SODRÉ

by P-06 Atelier
Designer – P-06 Atelier
Client – Lisbon City Hall, Lisbon Seaport, EDP

This lane runs along the Tagus River in Lisbon. Its 7362 meters cross different urban spaces, each one demanding a different solution. The goal was to define a new urban environment beyond the bikeway in order to improve this area along the river. The selection of compatible and existing materials was carefully considered in order to make clear the readability and use of the new system. The coating materials were used to strengthen the material unity that characterizes the space. This created a smooth and adherent surface that resembles Portuguese basalt pavement. In white paint, all the signs, symbols, and words establish boundaries, guidance, and information. The plan tells us a story, takes us, guides us, and seduces us along this route. As we continue, touristic, cultural, and natural points of interest are revealed through signage for transports, stops, or break points. It is in the use of Alberto Caeiro's poem about this river—the onomatopoeic intervention illustrating the sounds of the bridge—that exceed the basic needs of communication.

Typeface – Flama
Material ± Production – White paint stencils, graphic incisions made of metal circles and polygons filled with asphalt made over stabilized pavements
Project – P-06 Atelier together with GLOBAL, Landscape architecture
Director – Nuno Gusmão, João Gomes da Silva
Creative director – Nuno Gusmão, Pedro Anjos
Design team – Giuseppe Greco, Miguel Matos
Photographer – João Silveira Ramos, Giuseppe Greco

SUBSTITUT

by onlab
Designer – onlab
Client – Substitut Raum für aktuelle Kunst aus der Schweiz, Urs Küenzi

The non-profit art space, Substitut, is based in Berlin and commissioned onlab to create a visual identity for the space. The name "Substitut" implies being an institute as well as part of subculture. Drawing from this specific approach, onlab designed a multi-layer type design representing the visual identity of the art space.

Typeface – Sub (designed by onlab for Substitut)
Visual identity, art direction, design – onlab, Nicolas Bourquin, and Thibaud Tissot
Type design – Thibaud Tissot

ONDERNEMERSHUIS VAILLANTLAAN

by Studio Duel
Designer – Duel
Client – Municipality of The Hague

The office building Ondernemershuis (Center for Entrepreneurs) houses a number of companies that help entrepreneurs start their own businesses. The municipality of The Hague asked Studio Duel to design a complete identity. They developed a contemporary graphic pattern with an arabic twist, which forms the base for both the interior and exterior. The pattern was placed on more than 600 sqm of glass walls, doors, and floors. From the same forms that the pattern consists of, they made a typeface that was used for the inside and outside signage. Next to the artwork for interior and exterior, they unrolled a promotional printcampaign in the same graphic style.

Typeface – Homemade by Duel
Material ± Production – Print on transparent stickers
Architects – Roel Buijs
Photographer – Maarten Fleskens

TURBINE

by Studio Duel
Designer – Studio Duel
Client – Portaal

The Turbine is a new hotspot for freelancers in the communication sector. For the artwork for the Turbine, the designers of Studio Duel were inspired by the intriguing complexity of circuit boards and the industrial look and feel of the space. The 18 different work units are connected by a colorful graphic pattern. The Turbine-logo and interior signage blend in with the minimalistic architecture and interior design. In the far corner of the Turbine, they created a large blue surface that separates the work and lounge areas.

Typeface – Agrafa
Material ± Production – Paint, stickers
Interior design – Studio Überdutch and Renée Schuffelers
Photographer – Maarten Fleskens

KITA-SENJU MARUI SHOKUYUKAN

by Hiromura Design Office
Designer – Masaaki Hiromura
Client – Marui Co., Ltd.

Visual identity project for the 9th floor restaurants and food sections, as well as the 1st floor and basement of the Marui Department Store in Kita-senju, Tokyo. Pictograms were combined with the Chinese characters for food in order to convey the meaning in English. The signs were installed on the walls and corridors.

Interior – Chikara Shindou (Senjyumansai)
Photographer – Nacása & Partners Inc.

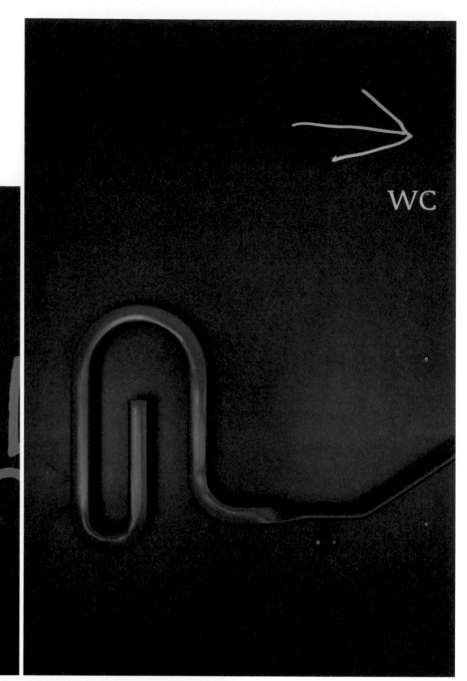

ELEMENTARY SCHOOL TSCHAGGUNS

by Sägenvier
Designer – Sigi Ramoser, Karoline Mühlburger
Client – Gemeinde Tschagguns

Lang Vonier Architects asked us to contribute our ideas and expertise in the field of signage and sign design for their project "Elementary School Tschagguns." We wanted to show what signage is able to contribute to a project; it can lead and orient people, reflect corporate identity, welcome visitors, communicate sympathy, and, sometimes, entertain. Including the pupils at the school was one demand for the project, therefore we assigned all kids from the kindergarden and the elementary school to draw signs, letters, and illustrations. They drew arrows, stairs, figures, tools, computers, and even birds for the 13 meters long glass façade, which connects the two buildings. We combined the kids' drawings and signs with a roman type. All elements are made of high quality foil, which were then stuck onto glass, wood, and concrete. There is not a single ordinary sign in the whole school. One funny detail was the tuba, which the kids drew for the music orchestra. We produced this object out of steel. To camouflage

the glass elements throughout the school building, we made a long list with over 400 professions—some of them are real and others are made-up. On the whole the project is very vitalized and bright!

Typeface – Parable
Material ± Production – Foil, metal
Architects – Lang Vonier Architekten ZT GmbH

PERCURSOS INACABADOS
(UNFINISHED TRAJECTORIES)

by R2 Design
Designer – Lizá Ramalho, Artur Rebelo
Client – Casa da Música

The installation was built in the north hall of Casa da Música and was the result of the reflection based on visitors' emotions and other viewpoints suggested by the spaces of the building. The objective was to list, classify, contextualize, build relations, and map the respective content. Experiences represented in various forms, which in turn generated a series of unfinished "scores" based on a wide array of details. The project aimed to question standard trajectories and propose new possibilities. The *Unfinished Trajectories* book formed part of the installation and served as a notebook for the assembled memories. An open book was placed on each step of the stairs. When the book was opened, a color stripe crossed over the book, extending to the surrounding space, leading to a succession of room-related words, centered with the stripe. New ways of discovering spaces thereby emerged, organized in alphabetical order, by scale, capacity, or other criteria. This was an unfinished project, delivering improbable—and sometimes absurd—itineraries.

Material ± Production – Vinyl
Photographer – Fernando Guerra

TEMPORARY GUIDING SYSTEM

by Vier5
Designer – Vier5
Client – Museum für Angewandte Kunst Frankfurt

Vier5 has been working on a new corporate design for the Museum für Angewandte Kunst Frankfurt. The museum was built by Richard Meier in the mid-1980s. During the 20 years of its existence, the museum has experienced several ups and downs in terms of its graphical appearance. The development of a corporate identity for a building the size of the Museum für Angewandte Kunst Frankfurt requires a lot of time and careful preparation, yet something referring to the upcoming identity change should be immediately perceivable. Sensible solutions for the guiding system were worked out together with the museum's staff and immediately implemented in the architecture and on the walls by means of felt-tip pens, and masking tape. In just a few days, a temporary design was created that could be quickly altered depending on the requirements. Changes in the museum thus became visible within a short period of time.

Material ± Production – Felt-tip pens, masking tape

Temporary orientation guides have become indispensable and extremely practical. We have been working on temporary, adaptable, and dynamic orientation guides since 2000. Our first project was the "Manifesta 4" in Frankfurt am Main, where we worked on a dynamic system to cover the whole of the city, including rest stops.

This type of orientation system is best used when the objective is to draw attention to something in the short term within a permanent or existing structure. Documenta, for example, has a very rigid timescale—everything needs to happen according to a timetable. Amongst all of that, there is a series of guest speakers (100 Tage, 100 Gäste) and there are often last-minute changes to this schedule that must be communicated to those visiting the event. This is only possible with temporary or adaptable orientation systems.

In 2004 we worked on a temporary system for the Museum für Angewandte Kunst in Frankfurt, where the aim was to clearly communicate to visitors from the outset that something was about to change in the museum. Our work needed to be visible; it was important to simulate a building site type of situation within the otherwise everyday routine of the museum.

Vier5

DEGREE SHOW 2006
UNIVERSITY OF APPLIED
SCIENCES DORTMUND

by RADAU – Gestaltung!
Designer – RADAU
Client – University of Applied Sciences Dortmund

At the University of Applied Sciences and Arts Dortmund, every year there is an exhibition at the end of every semester showing the final works of that year's graduating students. RADAU designed this exhibition in 2006. The theme for this exhibition was "assiduity"—a quality describing determined working. For the key visual the type was cut out of paper which, when done by hand, is a traditional and very industrious kind of work. Contrasting this are vibrant neon colors. Content of the cutouts were quotes from prominent people.

Typeface – Berlin Myriad, Kursivschrift Stehend,
Adobe Garamond, Dolly
Material ± Production – Neon paper, cardboard, tape
In cooperation with Nicole Kamasys
Photographer – Christoph Engel

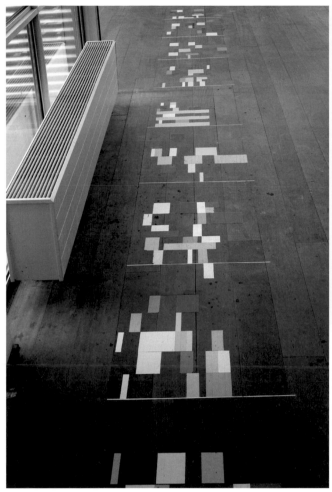

MEETING STRUCTURES

by Luna Maurer
Designer – Luna Maurer
Client – Museum De Paviljoens Almere, Netherlands

"Meeting Structures" (Overlegstructuren) is a project developed
for the exhibition "At Random? Netwerken en kruisbestuivingen" at
the Museum De Paviljoens, Almere, Netherlands from November
2007 to April 2008. During the course of the exhibition, the
designers taped the structures on the floor according to the
meeting agenda of the organization of the museum. The length
was about 40 meters. The white division lines indicate the weeks
that were subdivided into days. Vertically one day is displayed
from eight o'clock in the morning until ten o'clock in the evening.

Material ± Production – Tape on floor

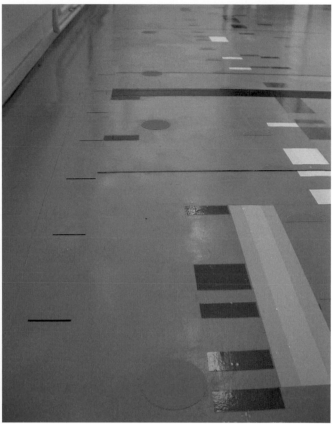

LIVING AGENDA

by Luna Maurer
Designer – Luna Maurer
Client – Museum Het Domein

Living Agenda was an installation during a one week residency
at the Museum Het Domein, Stittard, Netherlands in September
2005. The installation represents my agenda during the year
2005. Each color stands for a project, the red vertical stripes
indicate the months. Luna Maurer made the same installation for
the exhibition "Inside Out" at the Fonds BKVB in Amsterdam in
January 2006. This time the projects don't have a color code, but
the vertical position indicates what kind of project it is.

Material ± Production – Tape on floor

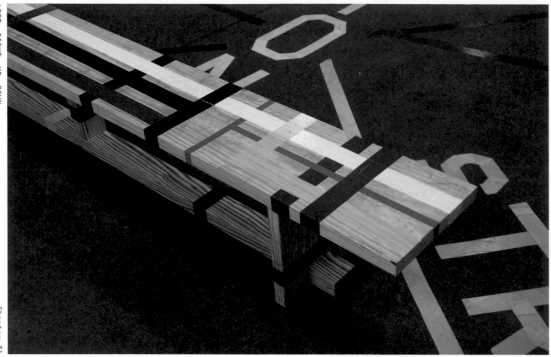

NIKE BENCH

by Melvin Galapon
Designer – Melvin Galapon
Client – Nike

Melvin Galapon was asked to embellish a bench, hand-built and designed by Max Lamb, with a sports related design. He decided to create the lines you would normally find in a school gymnasium.

Material ± Production – Tape on bench
Bench by Max Lamb
Photographer – Anne-Cecile Caillaud

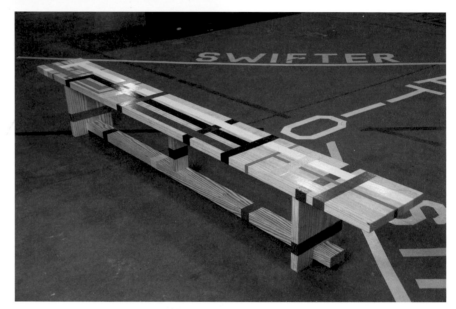

Sport-inspired decoration on specially commissioned bench.

NIEUW WONDERLAND – A MIND TWIST CAFÉ, PRINSENGRACHT 468, AMSTERDAM

by Matte
Designer – Matte, Meike Ziegler
Client – Meike Ziegler

Nieuw Wonderland is an experimental hospitality space where one becomes Alice in *Alice in Wonderland*, engaging in a curious new world of sensory experiences. A combination café, art gallery, and market place, Nieuw Wonderland is a place for the inquisitive to meet and connect with one another. Participants such as artists, chefs, and coaches, can try out new skills being a waiter for a day, serving food and drinks while touting their talents to visitors. Nieuw Wonderland provides a setting for conversation and exchange of ideas. An illustrator who represented the rabbit in *Alice in Wonderland*, painted a yellow line indicating time at Nieuw Wonderland. During his continuous four day performance, the movement of the line responded to the activities around him.

Typeface – Handwriting
Material ± Production – Yellow emulsion paint, illustrator
Illustrator/Performer – Esben Ingeslev
Photographer – Jeannine Govaers

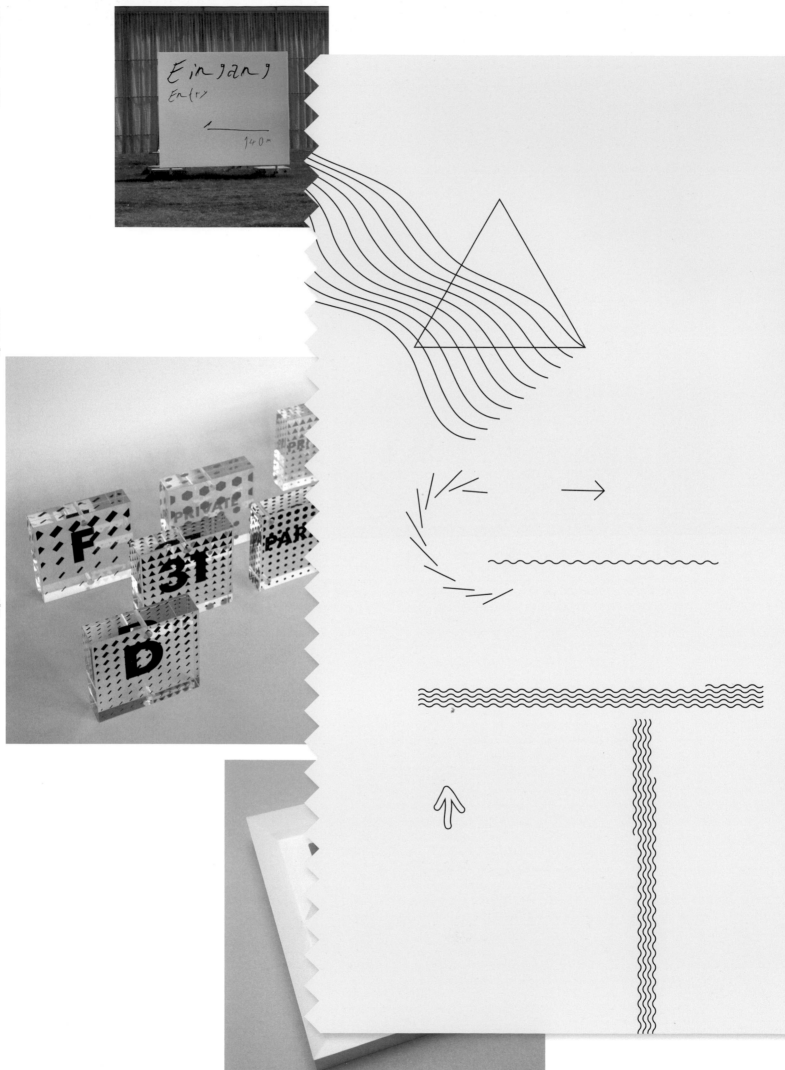

CHAPTER TWO
- MOUNTING BOARDS -

Photographer – Mark Whitfield. Material ± Production – Hand-woven tapestry

Material ± Production – Hand-woven tapestry

Material ± Production – Laser-cut letters and vinyl

Photographer – Ed Reeve. Material ± Production – Vinyl in between glass

Material ± Production – Vinyl in between glass

PARAMOUNT

by Mind Design
Designer – Mind Design
Client – Paramount

Paramount is a members' club and event space situated on the top three floors of one of the first skyscrapers in London. The concept for the identity is based on two main aspects: the architecture of the building and the notion of height. The logo consists of four different graduation patterns, which express an upwards movement. Variations of the design have been applied to different printed items, signage, and interior elements.

Typeface – Futura
Material ± Production – Screen-printed acrylic
Collaboration with Tom Dixon – Design Research Studio

A112B52

by Büro4
Designer – Büro4
Client – Fischer Liegenschaften Management, Zurich

Signage and wayfinding system for our office building in the heart of Zurich's city center (Kreis 4). The renovated industrial warehouse is located in the backyard, therefore it has two postal addresses: Ankerstrasse 112 and Bäckerstrasse 52. In addition to a distinctive information system, Büro4 designed two logos for the two main entrances: the anchor (as "Ankerstrasse" is the German word for "Anchor Street") and the pretzel ("Bäckerstrasse" is the German word for "Baker Street").

Typeface – Jigsaw Stencil (Typotheque, Peter Bil'ak)
Material ± Production – CNC-cut polyethylene PE300HD, paint on multiple surfaces, copper sheet

WALTER KNOLL
SIGNAGE SYSTEM AND BRAND LAND

by büro uebele visuelle kommunikation
Designer – Andrea Bauer, Katrin Dittmann, Andreas Uebele
Project manager – Marc Engenhart
Client – Walter Knoll AG&Co. KG

The signage system throughout the company works on two levels: one displays the brand, the other points the way. Both tasks are handled by a square module that varies in size, color, and angle, depending on its role. Brand world, bright red squares bear short sweet messages: upholstery; leather inspection; future. These signs accompany visitors as they enter the brand world, passing through the various buildings, which date from different centuries. These red signs, made of solid aluminum and set at 20 degrees from vertical, point to the brand's hallmark blend of high-tech production and traditional craftsmanship. They also pose little red riddles along the path throughout the brand world. The solutions are close-by, printed on large reflective surfaces. The texts on high-gloss aluminum plates explain, for example, how a machine works and the importance of the human hand, eye, and mind in inspecting the quality of the leather.

Signage system
The signs pointing the way through the buildings take the form of white type on aluminum plates of different sizes and are polished to a high gloss. Locational and directional signs appear large and small; the squares follow a matrix structure and figure in

different combinations in line with their architectural location. The cool sheen of the polished metal reflects the discreet understatement of the brand. The precision finish of the surface communicates the company's technical expertise. The pure design stands out against the various background surfaces, while the mirror-like material reflects the architectural image: bricks from the Gründerzeit, wooden panels in the joiner's shop, and fair-faced concrete in latest building. In all, the system merges with its surroundings without surrendering its identity. White and yellow squares communicate with the visitor. Temporary signage is handled by yellow squares set at an angle of 30 degrees to the vertical. These are held in place at the correct angle by hidden magnets milled into the reverse face of the backing plate. Information about the history of the older buildings on the site is displayed on small, bright, silver modules angled at 40 degrees. The reflective aluminum mirrors the language of the surrounding architecture, while the angled position echoes the new angle provided by the content. The screens provided for conference rooms play a visual rhythm of reflective stripes, and are applied to the glass with adhesive. The image of the onlooker melds and merges with the image of the room beyond the screen. The outcome is an irritatingly attractive pattern that detracts the attention from the people behind the screen without actually interrupting the line of sight.

Typeface – Frutiger Bold
Architects – Hansulrich Benz
Photographer – Andreas Körner

DOCUMENTA 12
GUIDING SYSTEM

by Vier5
Designer – Vier5
Client – Documenta

The guiding system, as understood by Vier5, has several levels and is viewed as a structure that can be divided into an informative, tangible, and abstract area: on one hand it is to be a functioning system that fulfills the visitors' primary wishes and leads them through the city to the desired places. On the other hand, the guiding system has another, uncontrollable and invisible function: it is meant to span a network and carry the aims and thoughts of the show to the outside, detached from the place and time of the exhibition—it is to evade a primary functionality.

Signs
The signs are meant to be in the way of the people in the city or the city zone and restrict the usual walking flow. Like with the containers, raw, pre-existing material is used. The bases of the signs are made of coarse concrete blocks which can also be found on building sites. The ceramic hills are the guards of the exhibition venues and indicate from the outside that one is standing in front of an exhibition venue. It is totally autonomous and greets the visitors at each exhibition venue in exactly the same position at the entrance of the building. In the year of the Documenta, many crown caps will line the ways and point to the direction that people and visitors will take through the city. Some of the crown caps will become buried in the earth and remain in the city for a long time to come. One of these crown caps was freed of its anonymity for Documenta 12; it was cast and gilded. It will be given back to the visitors of the show, who also become part of the guiding system, consciously or unconsciously, through their visit.

Typeface – Flaeche

300 Sozialwissenschaften
500 Naturwissenschaften

J000 – J900 MEDIATHEK

400 Sprache
600 Technik, Medizin, angw. Wiss.

GRUPPENARBEITSRÄUME

LESESAAL

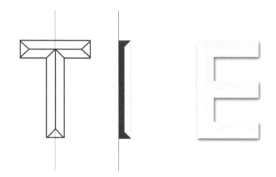

ABCDEFGHIJKLMNOPQRSTUVWXYZ
ABCDEFGHIJKLMNOPQRSTUVWXYZ
abcdefghijklmnopqrstuvwxyz
1234567890

Type: Blender Western Latin

Pictograms

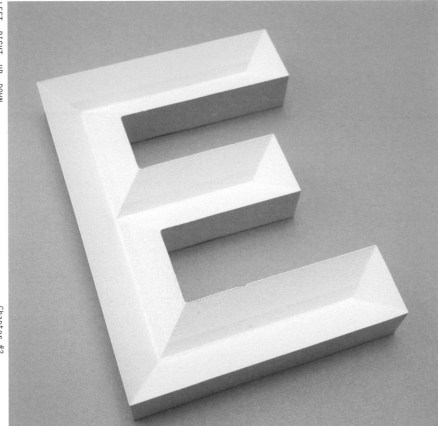

OBERÖSTERREICHISCHE LANDESBIBLIOTHEK LINZ (UPPER AUSTRIAN STATE LIBRARY, LINZ)

by bauer concept & design
Creative director – Erwin K. Bauer
Designer – Michael Herzog
Client – Oberösterreichische Landesbibliothek Linz

The building of the Upper Austrian State Library is a classical modernist structure dating back to the 1930s. An annex providing more space was built in 2009, the historical book storage building was opened to the public, and a modern media center was added as well. The orientation system makes a contemporary reference to the previous lettering: the *Antiqua* letters with their triangular profile that led to the rooms were replaced with white *Grotesk* lettering with an inverted profile, thus transforming their design for the digital age. The façade lettering was adjusted to match the institutions currently in the building. The replaced letters are now on exhibit as an historical artifact that reminds visitors of the original façade with the original name: Studienbibliothek. The information bearers that slant out of the wall are also an interpretation of the 1930s. White at the front, the color only reflects on the back when daylight falls on them. This accentuates the respective level designation. The direction is always shown intuitively by the shorter or longer slanted surface of the signs.

Typeface – Blender Western Latin
Material ± Production – Back-lit lasered metal pylons, folded lasered sheet metal sign, burned in lacquer with adhesive lettering
3D letters – Milled and lacquered synthetic material, adhesive material applied directly on the background
Architects – Bez & Kock
Photographer – Michael Herzog

SUPERTANKER

by Büro4
Designer – Büro4
Client – Swiss Life Property Management, Switzerland and Fischer Liegenschaften Management, Zurich, Switzerland

Logotype, signage, and wayfinding system for a large business building in the old Zurich industry area (Binz). The renovated warehouse was named SUPERTANKER as an homage to the enormous size of the building and to the distant view over Lake Zurich, which is visible from the newly built top deck offices.

Typeface – SUPERTANKER (Büro4, Dominik Wullschleger), Aaux (T26 Fonts, Neil Summerou)
Material ± Production – Mainly steel sheet or paint on multiple surfaces

UNIVERSITY OF APPLIED SCIENCES BERLIN
SIGNAGE SYSTEM

by Polyform
Designer – Polyform, Büro für Grafik- und Produktdesign
Client – Senatsverwaltung für Stadtentwicklung, Berlin
General architectural plan – Nalbach + Nalbach (Building B–G), Frank Augustin (Building A)

Openness, innovation, and communication, factors of the university's self-conception, influenced the conceptual design. The system is developed from the base element, which is a bubble—a square with rounded corners. According to the contents, this element is constantly changing into new shapes within a pattern. This creates a lively and open image on the premises. The two-dimensional effect and the floating impression of the elements in space emphasize the reduction of the orientation system to its pure communication purpose. The retaining constructions of the signs are clearly receded. The variety of colors and structures on the premises is contrasted with the system of white surfaces with black contours. Large-format direct signage in the interior accentuates the surface of the white walls. The basic appearance of the signage and information system remains monochrome.

Typeface – Accurat, Officina
Material ± Production – Sheet, steel

UNIVERSITY OF ARTS AND DESIGN KARLSRUHE (HFG) ORIENTATION SYSTEM

Designer – Sahar Aharoni, Johanna Bork, Patrizia Kommerell, Felix Vorreiter (Silvan Horbert joined the team until the first round of the competition) Mentor – Prof. Tania Prill Client – University of Arts and Design Karlsruhe

The HfG is housed in a former munitions factory and is therefore protected as a historic building. The new orientation system consisted of three components; door signs, directional signs, and orientation signs. Anodized aluminum door signs wrap around door frames without any mounting hardware. These signs have room numbers silk-screened directly on the metal. Directional signs feature large numerals that are easy to read from a distance, even in dim light. A modular system of orientation signage is mounted without screws on technical rooms at all exits. Information is permanent with the exception of a personnel register, which is refreshed every semester. Giant numerals and larger signs with more details indicate the current floor.

*Typeface – Simple
Material ± Production – Anodized aluminum signs, silkscreen printing
Pininfarina Förderpreis 2007*

OK, OFFENES KULTURHAUS OBERÖSTERREICH

by bauer concept & design
Creative director – Erwin K. Bauer
Designer – Angie Rattay, Michael Herzog
Client – OK Offenes Kulturhaus Oberösterreich

The interior and exterior wayfinding systems were developed for a new cultural hub consisting of two exhibition halls, restaurants, offices, and a large square in the historical center of Linz. It was necessary to take the existing historical buildings, contemporary architecture, and the surrounding urban space into account. The system, which uses embossed, spaced, and coated metal plates, reacts to all backgrounds and surfaces. White and grey are used in-house, while steel and black are used on the square.

Typeface – OK Stencil Wide (specially developed OK house font)
Material ± Production – Embossed and coated metal plates, adhesive material applied directly on the background
Architects – Riepl Riepl Architekten
Photographer – Philippe Gerlach

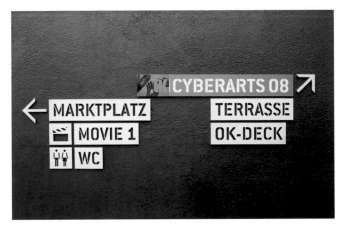

MILITARY TRAINING ACADEMY OF THE SWISS FEDERAL INSTITUTE OF TECHNOLOGY ZURICH, BIRMENSDORF

by Bringolf Irion Vögeli GmbH, Visuelle Gestaltung
Designer – Natalie Bringolf, Kristin Irion, Megi Zumstein
Client – Hochbauamt Kanton Zurich

With the arrival of the Military Academy, the Waffenplatz area was transformed into a training center. The conversion of the three buildings in the military barracks complex has significantly changed the atmosphere, light, and color of the interiors. A contemporary signage system had to do these changes justice. The orientation is defined by the room numbers that form the only constant element of the signage. They are reproduced as large aluminum numbers which are fixed directly onto the doors. The frequently changing functions of the rooms require a high degree of flexibility. To label the rooms, anodized aluminum letters can be put into tracked holding plates that are attached on the sides of the numbers.

Typeface – Kettler
Material ± Production – Aluminum numbers, anodized aluminum letters
Architects – Giuliani Hönger Architekten, Zurich
Technical realization in collaboration with Fokusform GmbH, David Weisser, Zurich
Photographer – Walter Mair, Zurich

ACE NYC DOOR SIGN

by The Official Mfg. Co.
Designer – Jeremy Pelley
Client – Ace Hotel New York

"This design was based on an old cigar label: simple, classic, timeless."

Typeface – Bauer Bodoni
Material ± Production – Gold foil, gold leaf, paint
Credits – Demitri Fregosi, Jack Barron, Alex Calderwood, The Official Mfg. Co.

EVERY EXIT IS AN ENTRANCE SOMEWHERE ELSE

by The Official Mfg. Co.
Designer – Fritz Mesenbrink, Mathew Foster, Jeremy Pelley, Johnne Eschleman
Client – Ace Hotel New York

"We were asked to do an art installation above the door, but the exit sign was in the way. So we embraced it and made it work. Success!"

Typeface – Helvetica Ultra Compressed
Material ± Production – Wheatpasted book pages, exit sign, paint

ACE NYC BATHROOM MIRROR MESSAGE

by The Official Mfg. Co.
Designer – Jeremy Pelley
Client – Ace Hotel New York

"Ace Hotel likes to have lots of special moments throughout the entire hotel, and this is just one of many."

Typeface – Found vintage type
Material ± Production – Screen print
Credits – Demitri Fregosi, Jack Barron, Alex Calderwood, The Official Mfg. Co.

ACE HOTEL PORTLAND WAYFINDING SIGN

by The Official Mfg. Co.
Designer – Jeremy Pelley
Client – Ace Hotel Portland

"Irwin-Hodson only had the hand that pointed to the left, so to make it work for the right, we had them flip it upside down (it was cheaper than getting a new one made). We thought it was funny and did the trick. Score!"

Typeface – Generic standard typeface
Material ± Production – Raw pressed steel
Credits – Philip Iosca, Jack Barron, Alex Calderwood, Irwin-Hodson Co.

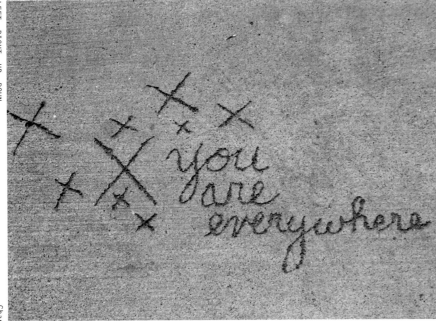

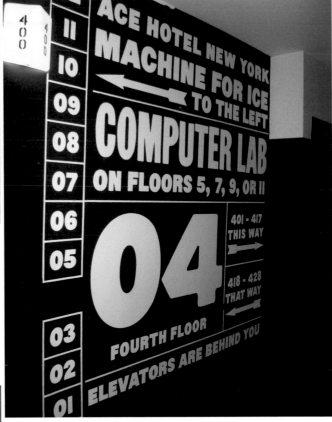

YOU ARE EVERYWHERE

by The Official Mfg. Co.
Designer – Jeremy Pelley
Client – Ace Hotel & Swim Club

"Funny story: I got in trouble for doing this at the time by one of the guys behind the build-out of the property. He was an idiot and I didn't feel bad about it because I knew it was awesome. Stick it, Manny."

Typeface – Hand drawn type
Material ± Production – Stick and wet concrete
Credits – The Official Mfg. Co., Connie Wohn

ACE NYC WAYFINDING MURAL

by The Official Mfg. Co.
Designer – Jeremy Pelley
Client – Ace Hotel New York

"We needed a creative solution for the wayfinding murals throughout the hotel, so we ran with a blend of the visual effects of vintage tickets and vintage subway signage. It allowed for us to add some humor into it as well."

Typeface – Black Gothic HPLHS
Material ± Production – Paint
Credits – Demitri Fregosi, Jack Barron, Alex Calderwood, The Official Mfg. Co.

ACE HOTEL PORTLAND EXTERIOR SIGN

by The Official Mfg. Co.
Designer – Jeremy Pelley
Client – Ace Hotel Portland

"Because of the historical society and regulations, we had the constraints of working with the original sign on the exterior of the building. The "hotel" neon was the only neon that still worked, so we let that lead the design. Funniest part: the neon bulbs on the edges are actually painted because they wouldn't let us remove it."

Typeface – Vintage/original
Material ± Production – Historical sign, neon, paint
Credits – Philip Iosca, Jack Barron, Alex Calderwood

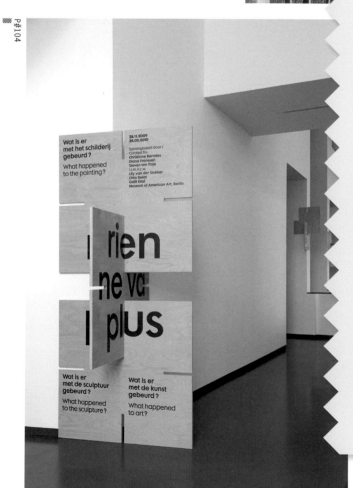

CHAPTER THREE
- SHAPING FORMS -

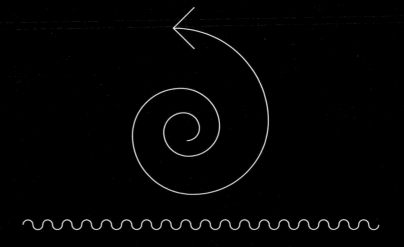

Close-up of auditorium signage.

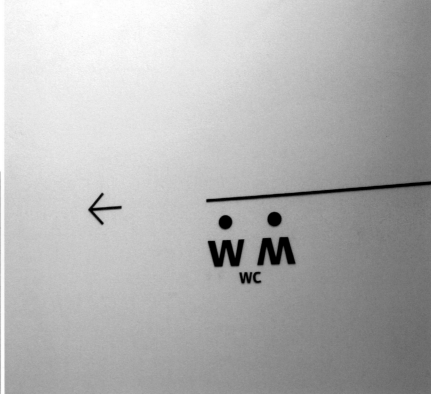

Bathroom signage.

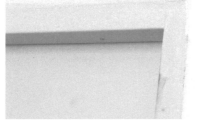

Office signage.

Outdoor sign for the center.

BEIRUT ART CENTER
(BAC)

by vit-e design studio
Designer – Nathalie Fallaha,
Khalil Halwani
Client – Beirut Art Center

Beirut Art Center (BAC) is a non-profit organization, space, and platform dedicated to contemporary art in Lebanon. The logo was created with the idea of pursuing a bilingual representation, while preserving a perfect equilibrium between the accent on both Arabic and English languages in the name. Hence both letters "B" in Latin and the Arabic letter "Baa" were integrated into one, resulting in a seamlessly integrated typographic solution.

Typeface – Foundry Form modified,
GE Dinar 2 modified
Material ± Production – Plexiglass laser cut
Photographer – Nathalie Fallaha

Ground-floor sign.

Bookstore signage.

CENTRAL SCHOOL OF SPEECH & DRAMA
IDENTITY, CAFÉ SIGN

by Studio8 Design
Designer – Studio8 Design
Client – Central School of Speech & Drama

Founded in 1906 and part of the University of London, Central's courses are held in high regard. The brief was to create an exuberant new identity that retained a sense of the school's heritage and prestige. A bespoke typeface family, produced with Dalton Maag, was created for the Central identity. It references old neon-lit theater signs. The project included external signage, internal wayfinding systems, posters, banners, and canvas bags.

Typeface – Fogerty (bespoke)
Material ± Production – Black perspex with white vinyl

TERM TIME OPENING
CAFÉ SERVICE
8.30AM – 4.00PM

———

BREAKFAST
8.30AM – 11.30AM

———

LUNCH
12.00 – 2.30PM

PICASSOHAUS UBS, BASEL

by Bringolf Irion Vögeli GmbH, Visuelle Gestaltung
Designer – Natalie Bringolf, Kristin Irion, Kristina Milkovic, Judith Stutz
**Client – UBS Fund Management, UBS Global Wealth Management &
Business Banking**

Doors of high-gloss-varnished olive wood, a rough slate floor, and the fanciful banisters
in the dominant staircase define the atmosphere in the heart of the office building. For the
logo at the entrance of the building and the meeting rooms, letters were cut from olive
wood and applied directly to the varnished olive wood surfaces. The differences in wood
grain contrast with the background surfaces make the letters visible. The different floors
in the building are marked with large ornamental lacquered chipboard numbers. The
numbers discreetly contrast with the background surfaces by means of their high-gloss
finish and the rawness of their uncoated cut edges.

Typeface – Bodoni Poster
Material ± Production – White lacquered chipboard, varnished olive wood
Architects – Peter Märkli Architekten, Zurich
Photographer – Walter Mair, Zurich

groundfloor
nmpb Architekten, Vienna

HUMANKIND ECONOMY TECHNOLOGY

by Ingeborg Kumpfmüller
Designer – Ingeborg Kumpfmüller
Client – University of Applied Sciences, St. Pölten

Humankind, economy, and technology describe the focus of the University of Applied Sciences. The installation of the signs begins in the outdoor area at the entrances and terraces and is continued in an interplay between signs that are upright, hovering, or set flush in the ground, from the entrance area to the foyer to frequented areas in the interior. They guide people in and around the building and through their presence give visual form to the content and structure of the university operation.

Typeface – Avenir
Material ± Production – Letters cut out of plexiglass
Architects – NMPB Architekten, Vienna
Photographer – Manfred Seidl, Vienna

Magnetic sheet, steel board.

Program agenda.

Outdoor simulation.

CINEMA ZUID

by Tenfinger
Designer – Tenfinger
Client – Muhka, Antwerp, Belgium

During the summer of 2009, Tenfinger was requested to conceive the new visual identity for Cinema Zuid in Antwerp. The outdoor sign produced in stainless steel material was intended as a three-dimensional identification for the institution before being developed and declined in a graphic form as a logo in the program agenda and all the communication tools.

Typeface – Akkurat

Austenitic stainless steel, handpolished.

Inside view simulation.

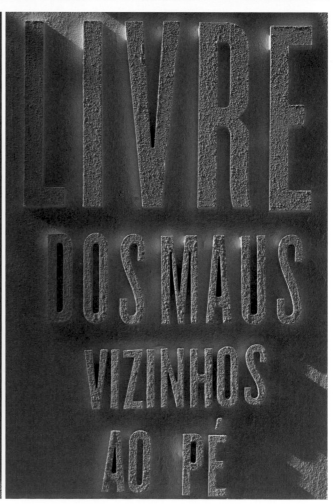

P#115

VAI COM DEUS
(GO WITH GOD)

by R2 Design
Designer – Lizá Ramalho, Artur Rebelo
Client – Ermida, Hermitage Nossa Senhora da Conceição

The Hermitage of Nossa Senhora da Conceição was built in Lisbon in 1707. Having reopened in 2008, this small chapel has since been used as a gallery for showing work by contemporary Portuguese artists. The gallery owner's main goal for the space was to make people aware of its reopening and its new purpose: drawing them to this new art gallery. One of the things that fascinated R2 Design was the chapel's original function as a place of worship. The dual presence of divinity and popular culture led the designers to play with idiomatic expressions in the Portuguese language that refer to God. They sought out formulae used by everyone which, by force of repetition, have become crystallized in the Portuguese language, while maintaining their status as conscious evocations of the divine. This collection of popular expressions highlighted the diversity of words, proverbs, and idiomatic expressions that are mechanically repeated by each one of us in our day-to-day lives. R2 Design used general expressions like: God is good and the Devil isn't so bad, space-evocative ones like: God save us from the bad neighbors on our doorstep and: When God closes the door, he opens a window. These were, respectively and appropriately placed next to the neighbor's façade and the other window. The texts were read by passers-by at different rhythms over the course of the day. Composed with *Knockout* typeface in the same color and texture as their background, letters, and words look as if they were coming out from the chapel's wall.

Typeface – Knockout by Hoefler & Frere Jones
Material ± Production – Waterproofed MDF sheets, sand paint
Photographer – Fernando Guerra

DOIS TEMPOS
(TWO TIMES)

by R2 Design
Designer – Lizá Ramalho, Artur Rebelo
**Client – Ermida, Hermitage Nossa
Senhora da Conceição**

Dois tempos (two times) is a reflection
on time and the current state of affairs,
achieved by means of a typographical
intervention on the façade of the old
Hermitage of Nossa Senhora da
Conceição, in Belém, Lisbon. This work
presents suggestive titles relating to
social, religious, political, economic,
and technological themes taken from
newspapers such as the *Diário de Notícias,
Jornal de Notícias, The Guardian, Le
Fígaro,* and the *New York Times.* A sense
of humor and strangeness is encountered
in unusual phrases: "Suspicious paper
bag closes Metro for two hours" (*Diário
de Notícias,* May 7, 2009): "World's
oldest woman dies happy" (*Jornal de
Notícias,* January 3, 2009) and: "Church
recommends seven days of sex" (in *Jornal
de Notícias,* November 25, 2008).
Countering the ephemeral and two-
dimensional nature of the original means of
communication (newspaper), the content
is re-presented at street level, with variable
luminosity and volume, on the building's
façade. The project may be seen on a 24-
hour basis, but with distinct appearances
at day and night. At night, the façade is
transformed into a huge light box where
the text is progressively separated from the
background by increasing its contrast and
legibility. The properties of the ink used
make it possible to emit light of varying
intensity that slowly fades over time. With
the aid of a torch, it is possible to intervene
in the installation, leaving a provisional
and individual record. This project is the
second of such typographical installations
produced by Artur Rebelo and Lizá
Ramalho in this space. The first intervention
(by the same designers) was presented in
September 2008.

*Typeface – Neutraface Slab,
House Industries
Material ± Production – MDF hydrofuge
sheets, fluorescent paint
Photographer – Fernando Guerra,
Tiago Pinto*

GRAPHIC DESIGN
FESTIVAL BREDA

by Rob van Hoesel
Designer – Rob van Hoesel + Yurr
Client – Graphic Design Festival Breda

The theme of the 2010 edition of this festival was "decoding." Present day digital as well as physical surroundings consist mainly of codes. The festival organization asked themselves what will happen if codes were dissected and altered. How do we experience our environment when codes are not (yet) known? Reprogramming of codes shows how humans function in an image-dictated society. The designers translated this theme by using a simple yet effective gesture; the folding. This folding visualizes the movement in the action of decoding images or messages. The folding is applied on both printed material, like posters, stickers, and the festival's catalog cover, as well as on the spatial signage that indicated the several locations of the festival. In every implementation the folding reveals the title of the festival "Decoding." Besides the simple gesture of folding, the effective use of fluor color makes the recognition even stronger.

Signage GDFB in the park.

GDFB headquarters in the House for Visual Culture.

GDFB signage at the House for Visual Culture.

Signage GDFB at the Graphic Design Museum.

GDFB signage at the House for Visual Culture.

PLAY VAN ABBE

by Tenfinger
Designer – Tenfinger
Client – Van Abbemuseum, Eindhoven

P#123

Opened on November 28, 2009, "Play Van Abbe" was a major exhibition project that ran for 18 months. A multi-faceted program, it worked with and around the collection of the Van Abbemuseum and covered the majority of the exhibition space. Tenfinger conceived an ever-changing signage and routing system. Wooden structures with directions, information, trigger quotes, and questions could be found throughout the museum. These were spread out and took on a viral character: always growing and changing.

Typeface – Toekomst
Material ± Production – Modules: CNC-cut plywood with UV-print
Photographer – Peter Cox

Material ± Production

Modules: CNC-cut plywood with UV-print

Seats: laser-cut polyurethane foam with coating

GIORGIO DE CHIRICO

by Studio Philippe Apeloig
Designer – Philippe Apeloig, Tino Graß
Client – Musée d'Art moderne de la Ville de Paris

Crisp line, dark shadow, and a similar color palette ran throughout
the work of Giorgio de Chirico in the exhibition "Giorgio de
Chirico la fabrique des rêves" at the Musée d'Art Moderne de
la Ville de Paris. The letter type and creation for the title greatly
reflect the qualities of the art. The font, *News Gothic,* mirrors the
sharp edges and definite separation between one object and
another. Giorgio de Chirico's use of space and extreme depth is
seen also in the title through dimension. With each letter raised off
the wall at different measurements, the title conveys the process
of layering in painting as well as creating strong shadows. By
creating the same contrast between shadow and color palette of
the paintings, this three-dimensional title gives way to the elements
of art within the paintings of Giorgio de Chirico.

Typeface – News Gothic
Material ± Production – Three-dimensional letters
Photographer – André Morin
Text – Rhapsody Valentine

THE ART INSTITUTE OF CHICAGO

by Pentagram Design Limited
Designer – Abbott Miller
Client – The Art Institute of Chicago

Pentagram designed the identity and environmental graphics for the Art Institute of Chicago, the second largest art museum in the U.S. The project was timed to the completion of the institute's new $294 million Modern Wing, a 24,525 m^2 expansion designed by the Pritzker Prize-winning architect Renzo Piano that opened in May 2009. The graphics integrate the museum's historic past with its re-energized present. The new identity was inspired by the inscription of the museum's name on the entry façade of its original 1893 Beaux Arts building. The inscription uses the Roman "V" in place of the "U" in the word "Institute" and has become a graphic signature for the museum. Pentagram's signage has been fully integrated with the architecture of Piano's addition, using materials of aluminum, stone, and glass and elements of inscription and transparency. During planning, the designers discovered that the words "The Art Institute of Chicago" fit exactly within the mullions at the crown of Piano's addition. In the finished installation, these letterforms sandwich the plate glass and appear to float in air. The team also completed a complete program of wayfinding, directories, and donor signage for the entire museum.

Art director – Abbott Miller
Designers – Abbott Miller, Jeremy Hoffman, Kristen Spilman,
Susan Brzozowski

CHILDREN'S MUSEUM OF PITTSBURGH
ENVIRONMENTAL GRAPHICS

by Pentagram Design Limited
Designer – Paula Scher
Client – Children's Museum of Pittsburgh

Pentagram created playful signage and environmental graphics
for an expansion of the Children's Museum of Pittsburgh.
Designed by Koning Eizenberg Architecture, the expansion links
the museum's home in the landmark Old Post Office Building
with the neighboring, vacant Buhl Planetarium. The structure is
crowned with a shimmering wind sculpture made of thousands
of plastic tiles that move in the breeze. Like the architecture, the
signage helps establish an atmosphere of exploration and activity
at the museum. The entrance marquee appears in dimensional
letterforms reminiscent of superhero comics, and the donor wall
in the lobby is composed of colorful fluorescent plexiglas panels.
Throughout the museum, the signage utilizes inexpensive materials
and fixtures that can be easily repaired or replaced.

Art director – Paula Scher
Designers – Paula Scher, Rion Byrd,
Andrew Freeman
Photographer – Peter Mauss/Esto

INGELSTA SHOPPING

by BVD
Creative director – Carin Blidholm Svensson
AD/Graphic designer – Kina Gisenfeld Herner
Project manager – Mia Hesselgren
Project-/production manager – Gunilla Orander
Client – Eurocommercial Properties

Assignment
Ingelsta Shopping concept and communication. Strategy, name, graphic identity and manual, exterior and interior signage and wayfinding system, campaign communication platform, launch campaign. March 2008 – September 2009.

Challenge
To create a complete concept to re-profile the shopping center in Norrköping.

Solution
The concept was based on the idea "communication to the big and little," which was executed on all levels. The graphic identity has, for example, two symbols: a large and small dot. Additionally, all signs were designed to communicate in duplicate—one message at adult eye-level and one at eye-level for children. The mascot "Inge" was created and, along with his companion characters, placed in the environment and on printed material. The kids even got their own toilet, café tables, and menu with mini-cinnamon buns.

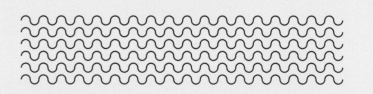

CHAPTER FOUR
– DEFORMING SHAPES –

ARCHITECT | ARQUITECTO VENTURA TERRA | 1866—1919

by P-06 atelier
Designer — P-06 atelier
Client – Assembly of the Portuguese Republic

Graphic and environmental project for the exhibition "Architect | Arquitecto Ventura Terra | 1866–1919." Ventura Terra, a well-known Portuguese architect from the 19th century, was the author of the project for the building of the Assembly of the Portuguese Republic, in which the exhibition was held. The target audience was the general public, tourists, and portuguese citizens, so the designers were asked to make a strong announcement due to the importance of the architect in Portugal and because renovation had finished in the building. An exterior announcement was made as a "signature" of the author of the project. This could be viewed by everyone who passed on the street. The technical solution was the cheapest material they could get: adhesive vinyl stretched and laid down the stairs.

Typeface – Flama
Material ± Production – Black adhesive vinyl stretched and laid down the stairs
Creative director – Nuno Gusmão
Project – Nuno Gusmão, Estela Pinto, Pedro Anjos
Designers – Vera Sachetti, Giuseppe Greco, Miguel Matos
Photographer – Francisco Feio
Fabricators – Eurostand

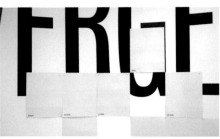

At the time of the exhibition's opening in August 2009, only about half of the participating artists and architects had submitted places for inclusion in the exhibition. Throughout the following 12 months, the remaining contributions were to be added. The design scheme had to account for the fact that only half of the content would be available at the beginning, be flexible enough to allow for the gradual inclusion of the rest during the run of the show, and inexpensive and easy to maintain.

CONVERGENCE 142

by Neil Donnelly
Designer – Neil Donnelly
Client – Ordos Museum of Art, Ordos, Inner Mongolia, China

Each of the 100 architects participating in the Ordos Project, an architectural commission in Ordos, Inner Mongolia, China, as well as the 42 artists whose works are included in the Ordos Museum of Art's collection, were invited to describe a place in their city of special significance: a slip in the urban fabric that betrays something secret or suppressed, or simply overlooked; something curious and unexpected, something that in the eyes of each author offers a nuanced insight into the identity of their city.

Typeface – Bureau Grotesque, Hei
Material ± Production – Inkjet printing on paper, vinyl letters
Curators – Joseph Grima and Beatrice Galilee

One sheet of paper, fluorescent pink on one side and white on the other, was assigned to each contributor. The contributor's name was printed on the white side and then hung on the title wall, obscuring the show's name. When a contribution was received, the corresponding sheet was removed from the title wall and the contribution was printed on the pink side. Then the sheet was hung, pink side out, in a geographically appropriate place in the exhibition (large longitude numbers turned the walls into a kind of global map), immersing the viewer in a world created by the exhibition's participants.

KUNSTRASEN 08

by Nagelprobe / David Nagel
Designer – Lucas Gerber, David Nagel

This signage system was part of an entire corporate design
for Kunstrasen 08—a soccer world cup of art schools in 2008
organized and designed by students of the University of the
Arts Bremen. The cup itself was meant to communicate a kind
of archetype soccer vibe, therefore the signage system used the
method of marking the soccer playing field with chalk. It also had
to meet different demands: on one hand it needed to be low cost
and easy to produce; on the other hand temporary and gentle to
the soccer ground.

Typeface – Avenir Next
Material ± Production – Chalk, grass
Kunstrasen 08 team – Alexander Böll, Johannes Ellmer,
Lucas Gerber, Daria Groß, Matthias Keller, David Nagel,
Allegra Schneider, Steffen Vogt

ÉCOLE ESTIENNE PARIS
ENTRY SIGNAGE

by Toan Vu-Huu
Designer – Baldinger•Vu-Huu
Client – École Estienne Paris

The signage guides the students with its red line from the main road to the principle entry of the school. It is the declination of the visual identity concept with a flexible logo.

Typeface – Custom drawn
Material ± Production – Red sign color on asphalt

GREY GROUP

by Pentagram Design Limited
Designer – Paula Scher
Client – Grey Group

A creative company needs an innovative workspace. For Grey Group, one of the largest marketing communications companies in the world, a move to a new, state-of-the-art headquarters in the former International Toy Center in the Flatiron District, a New York design hub, symbolized a renewed commitment to creativity. The designers developed an inventive program of environmental graphics for the offices. The graphically playful signage promotes the creativity of the company's various divisions and at the same time ties the loft-like floors of the new headquarters together into a cohesive environment. The interiors were designed using different materials for each division or department on each floor. The environmental graphics use these same materials—wood, glass, metal, and polymer—in ways that suggest the personalities of the different divisions. The signage mixes the materials with elements of reflection, transparency, lighting, and pattern to create a series of optical illusions that sets each department apart. Visitors to the first floor lobby are greeted by a front desk backed by a dramatic wall of backlit metal mesh that features both the logos of Grey Group and G2 rendered in the same mesh. For the open, gallery-like spaces of the second and third floors, which contain Grey's creative departments, the designers created large-scale installations that brand the agency in the space. The second floor features large windows on Madison Square Park and distressed elements like exposed brick that remain from the building's previous incarnation. Here, the designers created a typographic neon sculpture with the Grey logo rendered inside a 35" cube that sits on the floor like a piece of art. Surrounded by reflective glass, the cube activates the space. Restrooms on the second and third floors feature anamorphic superscale male and female icons that appear "correct" at their respective entrances but then graphically stretch down the halls.

Art director – Paula Scher
Designers – Paula Scher, Andrew Freeman

EUREKA CARPARK

by Axel Peemöller
Designer – Axel Peemöller
Client – Emery Studio

In Melbourne Axel Peemöller developed a wayfinding system for the Eureka Tower Carpark while working for Emery Studio. The idea was to create an exciting space with functionality. The space was disorienting, which led to designing a wayfinding system that was both visually beautiful and graphically challenging. The distorted letters on the walls can be read perfectly when standing at the right position. This provides the essential information at the right time and location when it is needed; unnecessary information creates a beautiful chaos of distorted graphical elements at the same position.

RE

by Yoshimaru Takahashi
Designer – Yoshimaru Takahashi
Client – Osaka University of Arts

"Re" means to reproduce like recycling or regeneration. The typography on the wall surfaces means that a green life is reproduced on the surface of concrete walls when it is viewed from the right position. The typography is designed on the wall surface so as to materialize two-dimensional typography in three-dimensional space.

Typeface – Helvetica Bold
Material ± Production – Artificial grass
Supported by GD Research Workers of Osaka University of Arts Graduate School

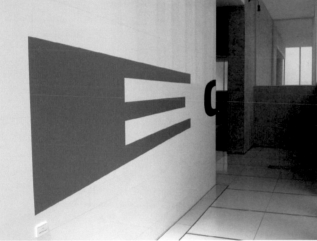

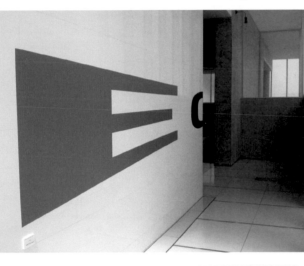

07-ECO$_2$

by Yoshimaru Takahashi
Designer – Yoshimaru Takahashi
Client – Osaka University of Arts

The CO$_2$ problem is a major problem for the ecology of the Earth. The typography on the wall surface expresses that the CO$_2$ problem and ecology are the same when it is viewed from the same position. The typography is designed on the wall surface so as to materialize two-dimensional typography in three-dimensional space.

Typeface – DIN
Material ± Production – Cutting sheet
Supported by GD Research Workers of Osaka University of Arts Graduate School

08-ECO$_2$

by Yoshimaru Takahashi
Designer – Yoshimaru Takahashi
Client – Osaka University of Arts

"08-ECO$_2$" is the continuation of "07-ECO$_2$." This project by Yoshimaru Takahashi, based on three-dimensional typography, draws attention to the ecological CO$_2$ problem. Depending on the viewer's perspective, the displayed words or abbreviations alter their meanings. "08-ECO$_2$" can be read either as "ECO$_2$" or "EGO."

Typeface – DIN
Material ± Production – Cutting sheet
Supported by GD Research Workers of Osaka University of Arts
Graduate School

09-ECO2

by Yoshimaru Takahashi
Designer – Yoshimaru Takahashi
Client – Osaka University of Arts

Depending on the angle, the sign of the work can be read as "ECO" or "CO$_2$."

*Typeface – Original
Material ± Production – Cutting sheet
Supported by GD Research Workers of Osaka University of Arts
Graduate School*

C2

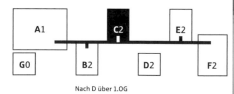

Nach D über 1.OG

KREISSPARKASSE LUDWIGSBURG

by L2M3 Kommunikationsdesign GmbH
Designer – Frank Geiger, Sascha Lobe
Client – Kreissparkasse Ludwigsburg

The conceptual design of a functional and beyond that, identity-building guidance system. The savings banks, acting independently of one another, are each searching for their own local reference. For Ludwigsburg, on one hand, the conceptual approach "baroque," with its architecturally mediated delusions of the eye, is definitive for the main design theme; on the other hand, it is the architectural characteristic of a 140 meters long access corridor that ties together the various new buildings. The labelings of the floors and staircases are pre-distorted by means of perspective so that from one point only they can be correctly perceived and otherwise change into free plays of form.

Typeface – Sparkasse
Architects – KBK Architekten Belz | Lutz
Photographer – Florian Hammerich

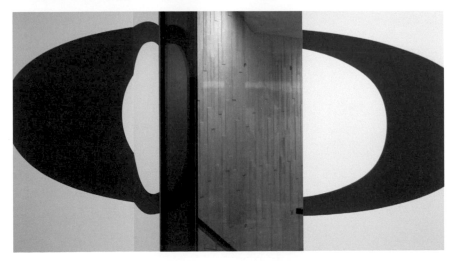

THE COOPER UNION

by Pentagram Design Limited
Designer – Abbott Miller
Client – The Cooper Union

Pentagram designed signage and environmental graphics for
the Cooper Union's new academic building designed by the
Pritzker Prize-winning architect Thom Mayne of Morphosis and
located on Cooper Square in Manhattan's East Village. The
program included identification, wayfinding, and donor signage
and is fully integrated with the building's innovative architecture.
The building canopy features optically extruded lettering that
appears correct when seen in strict elevation, but distorts as the
profile of the letter is dragged backwards in space. An ambitious
installation of donor signage is displayed above the stairway that
descends through the "vertical piazza" in the building's center.
The building opened in September 2009.

Art director – Abbott Miller
Designers – Abbott Miller, Jeremy Hoffman, Brian Raby,
Susan Brzozowski
Photographers – Chuck Choi, Iwan Baan

Back wall at Kellen Auditorium. Photographer – © Noah Sheldon

Back-lit signage at Kellen archives. Photographer – © Michael Moran

Bathroom signage. Photographer – © Lyn Rice Architects

SHEILA C. JOHNSON DESIGN CENTER

by Lyn Rice Architects
Designer – Lyn Rice Architects
Client – The New School

Overview
The Sheila C. Johnson Design Center establishes a new 2,900 sqm campus nexus for Parsons The New School for Design by uniting and comprehensively re-organizing the street-level spaces of the school's four buildings around a new urban quad. The center performs as an expansive urban threshold that draws together the school's creative programs and their vibrant Greenwich Village context.

Graphics strategy
Merge graphics and architecture at the SCJDC, graphic content and architectural strategies are conceived together in a way that reinforces both. Graphics are neither physical nor conceptual add-ons; these graphics have integrated architectural functions performing as spatializer, texturizer, material-enhancer, illuminator, protector, teacher, time-keeper, and acoustic-controller, in addition to the roles of wayfinding, branding, and identity. Graphic canopies two new campus entries were created for the project and are importantly signified by twin, 15 meters long graphic canopies stretching east-west along West 13th Street, and north-south along Fifth Avenue where, according to New York City zoning rules, signage height is limited to three neters. The signage at these important access points needed to operate at an urban scale (the existing buildings are twelve stories tall) and by tipping these tightly spaced, three-dimension aluminum block letters on their sides, the installation achieves a large scale, meets the zoning requirement, and in the rotation, creates a memorable branding of the school and defines an exterior space at each entry as a protective canopy.

5th Avenue entry with graphic canopy. Photographer – © Michael Moran

The identity set-up

Exposing a graphic interior for a university with a diverse range of creative programs, the issue of identity is complex and for the SCJDC, identity is not so much imposed as it is revealed and staged. LRA worked as identity planners—setting up opportunities for the students to create the character of the center with their own work. LRA resisted the impulse to represent design through formal elements at the facade and instead sought solutions that place the academic work on display. At the complex's perimeter, a series of new large-panel, deep-set, aluminum-framed windows are shingled in plan (rotated toward the intersection) and tilted out in section (toward the sidewalk) to allow expanded views to and from the street. The primary view is not of the façade, but rather through it to the exhibited student work inside. An aluminum armature spans vertically within the deep frame nearest the entry, supports a series of independent, glowing, 80 cm deep, hand-cut, solid acrylic letters that form the name of the center.

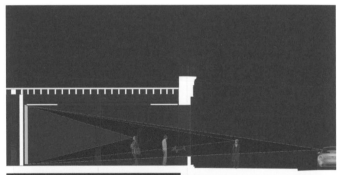

Street section diagram. Photographer – © Lyn Rice Architects

Pedagogical billboards

Integrating student work in the architecture LRA programmed the complex's three existing elevator/stair cores as graphic surfaces for exhibiting Parsons' student work at an urban scale. These graphic pedagogical billboards will be updated periodically with new work drawn from the diverse range of Parsons' art and design programs, including architecture, communication design, digital design, fashion design, fine arts, graphic design, interior design, photography, and product design. Student works are adapted for installation or conceived specifically as part of a studio curriculum, so that the graphic cores become sites where critical inquiry meets real world conditions. Outcomes range from the subtle and bodily intimate to the graphically monumental, with each student installation holding the power to alter the space's character and mood.

Typeface – Impact
Material ± Production – Welded aluminum letters on steel structure

View of light box wall from exterior. Photographer – ©Lyn Rice Architects

View of Welcome Center through security threshold. Photographer – ©Lyn Rice Architects

View through security threshold. Photographer – ©Lyn Rice Architects

Movable panels of light box wall. Photographer – ©Lyn Rice Architects

13th Street entry with graphic canopy. Photographer – ©Lyn Rice Architects

Kellen archives. Photographer – ©Michael Moran

ARRISCAR O REAL
(RISKING REALITY)

by R2 Design
Designer – Lizá Ramalho, Artur Rebelo
Client – Berardo Collection Museum

The "Arriscar o Real" (Risking Reality) exhibition focuses on various artists who have explored the mimesis of reality and transformed this question into a paradox. Divided into three sections with corresponding spaces, the dominant concept was associated to the meaning of the real and figurative in space. The exhibition's design was not restricted to a merely informative aspect; it directly intervened in the museum's space. The typography— normally associated with a two-dimensional format—was materialized in the form of a genuine object of design. R2 Design attempted to use color to guide visitors' movements through the exhibition. The impact of red in the entrance hall was progressively attenuated through recourse to shades of grey, applied in the different sections of the museum. In this manner, the visitor's itinerary evolved from darker to lighter shades. Three-dimensional letters were placed on the entrance hall floor, forming the words "Arriscar o Real." However the manner in which these letters were read altered in accordance to the observer's viewpoint. The letters were red—like the color of the museum's entrance hall—and the public could lean against them while admiring the works of art.

Material ± Production – Vinyl, MDF hydrofuge sheets
Photographer – Fernando Guerra

DOCKS EN SEINE, CITÉ DE LA MODE ET DU DESIGN (FASHION AND DESIGN CENTER)

by Nicolas Vrignaud
Designer – Nicolas Vrignaud
Client – Icade

The signage intervention in the building Docks en Seine plays with the usual needs of signage and with the context. The building is a sign; it participates in the urban renewal of the 13th district of Paris and it becomes one moment along the Seine, as a sequence, a cursor. This signage project is based on this idea of sequence and also on the idea of promenade, of wandering. The pre-conception of this signage project is to punctuate this horizontal movement by beacons, and to create a declension on four levels from the access at the bank level of the Seine towards the rooftop. The fact of preserving and renovating the existing building while keeping the concrete structure, offers support to the signage system, which is as a moulding of this structure, creates a new relationship to the architecture. It takes place at different points: circulation, shop, communication, etc. These moulds, called "plugs," are separated from their support to become independent. Every plug is in aluminum and unique. They are grouped by type according to their application. The plugs are used like billboards all along the building and the graphic design, in opposition to the plugs, could evolve according to the visual identity.

Typeface – Grotesque
Material ± Production – Aluminum

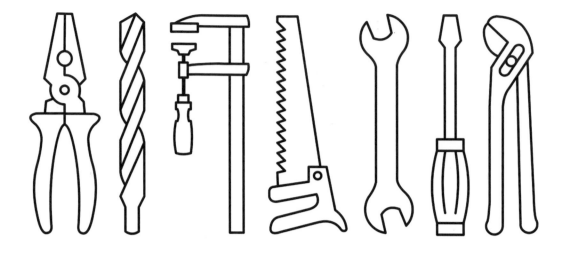

VIERINGHAUSEN 0,1 km
GRILLPLATZ

KREMENHOLL 0,95 km
PARK

HAUPTBAHNHOF 2,0 km

DEUTSCHES
WERKZEUGMUSEUM 2,9 km

SPIELFLÄCHE
HASTEN 2,0 km

AUSSICHTSPUNKT
STOCKDEN 0,65 km

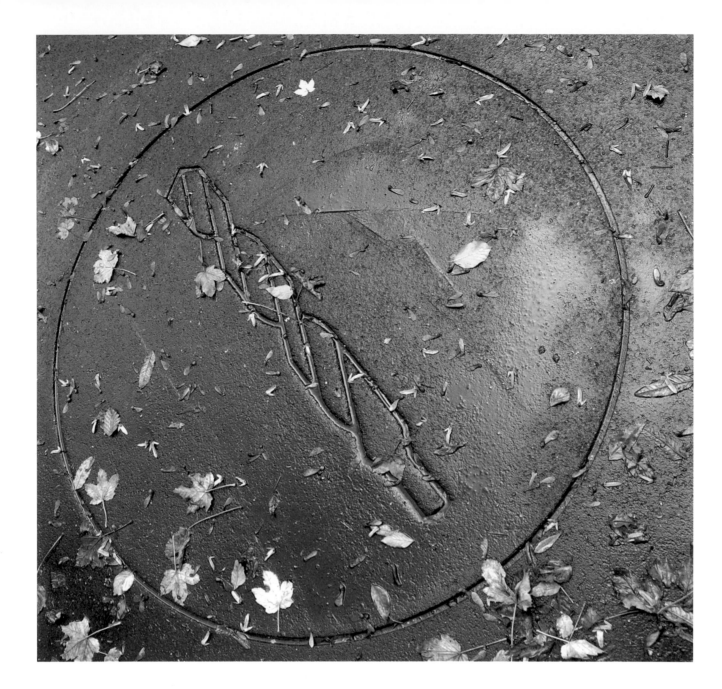

TRASSE DES WERKZEUGS
(ROUTE OF TOOLS)

by Kalhöfer & Rogmans
Designer – Kalhöfer & Rogmans
Architects – Kalhöfer-Korschildgen
Client – Stadt Remscheid

The project consists of old railroad tracks that had been transformed into a pedestrian/
cycle path. The town of Remscheid is famous for its tools, so everything along the route
is related to that theme; along the way you will find some graphic interventions around
that theme such as markings and embossings. These elements were also necessary to
connect the route, which goes through heterogenous and to some extent very derelict
districts. Graphic design was the only possibility to make the route identifiable as such,
even over 4.5 km. The small budget prompted us to emphasize upon graphic design. In
addition to the graphic design, several parks were planned. Two of them were made:
Remscheid-Hasten and Remscheid-Kremenholl.

Typeface – Trade Gothic Bold
Material ± Production – Premark® thermoplastic road marking
Assistant – Daniel Angulo García
Photographer – Marc Rogmans

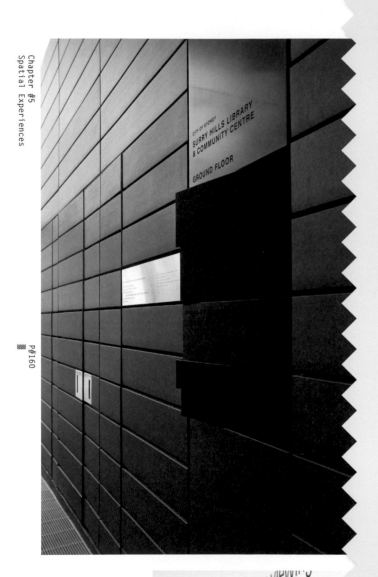

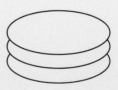

CHAPTER FIVE
- SPATIAL EXPERIENCES -

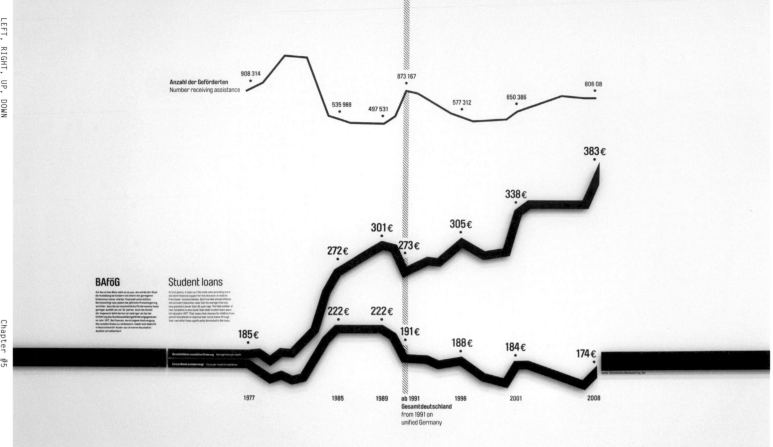

Anzahl der Geförderten
Number receiving assistance

908 314

535 969   497 531

873 167

577 312   650 386   806 08

383 €

338 €

301 €   305 €

272 €   273 €

BAföG   Student loans

222 €   222 €

185 €   191 €   188 €   184 €   174 €

Durchschnittliche monatliche Förderung   Average loan per month

Darlehen/Rückzahlung   Loan/repayment

1977   1985   1989   ab 1991
Gesamtdeutschland
from 1991 on
unified Germany   1996   2001   2008

4 280 630

3 698 057

3 246 727
3 007 142

2 228 004   2 498 392   2 378 918

Arbeitslosigkeit
Unemployment

1 868 504

1 883 147

1 073 576   1 074 217   876 137

459 489

154 523

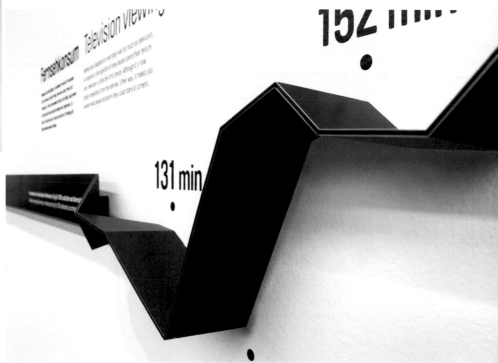

STATISTICS STRIP IN THE EXHIBITION "WORK. MEANING AND WORRY"

by ART+COM AG
Designer – ART+COM
Client – German Hygiene-Museum Dresden

Like the handrail of a staircase that leads step by step up or down, the statistics strip leads the visitor through the exhibition "Work. Meaning and Worry," shown in the German Hygiene-Museum Dresden. The idea was to create a thread guide through the exhibition that deals with the function and meaning of work for people and the society. As the unifying element, the black aluminum strip extends across all rooms and places the exhibits in the greater context. It folds along the wall and widens into object-like graphs and charts of various types: 3D lines, surfaces, columns, beams, and dots show extensive, transparent, and easy to understand background information, and amazing details. The greater the numbers, the bigger the display on the wall; some charts spread over three meters in height. All graphs are labelled with typeface wall graphics and some are provided with extra information. In addition, seven interactive media stations with projections are integrated into the strip, where visitors can change different parameters by turning knobs and thus retrieve various data. 50 small monitors contrast the figures on the wall with individual perspectives; using touch screens, interviews with over 100 people are embedded into the statistics strip.

Material ± Production – Aluminum Dibond

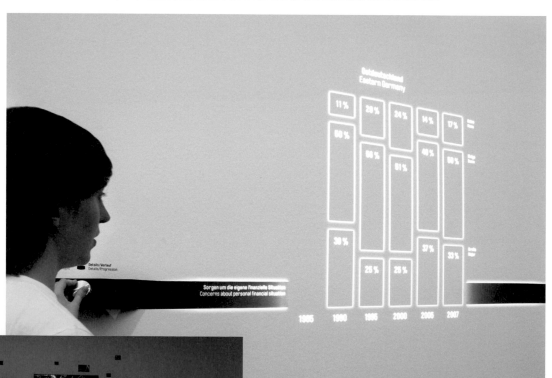

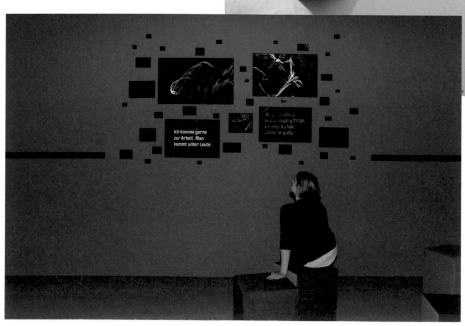

Konsumausgaben

Wie es sich für eine kapitalistische Wohlstandsgesellschaft gehört, steigt der Konsum seit Jahrzehnten an. Diese Entwicklung ist auch eine Geschichte der zunehmenden Bedeutung von Dingen, die für das Überleben zunächst nicht unmittelbar notwendig scheinen – wie zum Beispiel Reisen und Telekommunikation. Im Vergleich zur Grundversorgung mit Ernährung und Kleidung wird hierfür Jahr für Jahr mehr Geld ausgegeben.

Consumer spending

As it should be in an affluent capitalist society, consumption has been rising for decades. This development is also a history of increasing importance of items that do not initially appear necessary for immediate survival – such as travel and telecommunications. In comparison to basic needs such as food and clothing, more money is spent on these things every year.

Anstieg der Konsumausgaben der privaten Haushalte
Rise in consumer spending by private households

1970   1980   1990   2000   2007

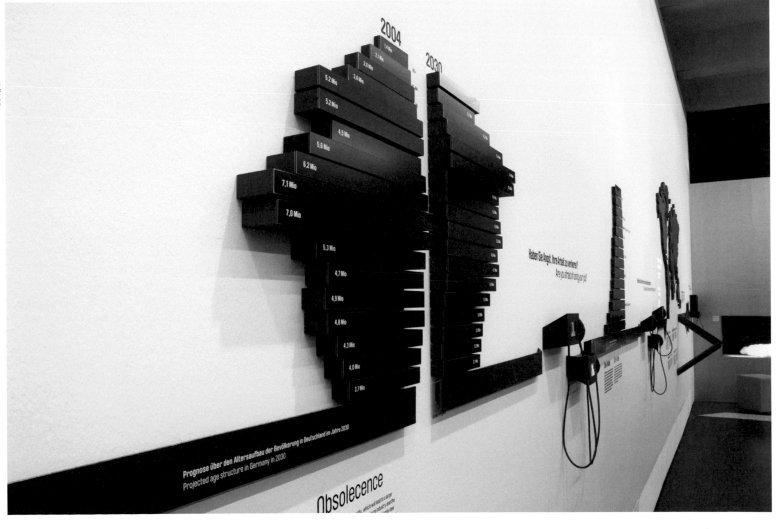

2004   2030

Prognose über den Altersaufbau der Bevölkerung in Deutschland im Jahre 2030
Projected age structure in Germany in 2030

Obsolecence

SURRY HILLS LIBRARY & COMMUNITY CENTER

by Andrew van der Westhuyzen
Designer – Andrew van der Westhuyzen & Clemens Habicht
Client – City of Sydney

The designers aimed to honestly engage with and be sympathetic to the architects' vision. Like the building, the identity and signage needed a contemporary sense of place and a strong connection to its setting. It should be inviting, and like the building, quiet in its relationship to its context.

Emergence/submergence
The interface between the library and the public space on the south wall is an important integrated community environment. In the building's design there is a blurring of the distinction between the interior and exterior. Even the offsetting of the building from the footpath implies a reverence to public space. Andrew van der Westhuyzen and Clemens Habicht's typographic treatment reinterprets the physicality of the identity as an extrusion/ intrusion of surfaces throughout the building. The internal angled glass wall is an important functional architectural feature of the building and its climate system. This bio-filtration atrium is such a visually prominent and important feature that it became the starting point. It influenced the visual presentation of the type embedded in the surfaces; extruded type or the fields on which they occupy, are similarly angled against vertical wall structures in homage to this architectural feature. Through this the designers aimed to create a strong, important interaction between the facility and the community.

Address the public Important for the designers is that the identity of this building is given prominence in the public eye and this can only be achieved by being respectful to the observer. With this concept, typography is turned to the viewer: like a tilt of the head or an old fashioned dip of a hat, the skewed axis of the signage is aimed to face different people, giving attention and an audience to the public.

Permanence and integration
With the bio-filtration atrium being such a visually prominent and important feature, it became the starting point. The designers intend the signage to have the quality of longevity by treating them as fittings rather than appendages or stickers. They feel part of the same mould as the building itself, so that one does not feel complete without the other. Beyond titling and wayfinding, the signs also need to communicate a permanence in the building's function as a library and community center. Permanence as an identifiable value will assist in an ownership by the community it serves; it is a dedicated library and community center and will remain so. There should not be a feeling of transience that results from a technology applied merely to the surface that can and might be changed. The type is an expression of the building's design by utilizing the material of the surface it is on. Embedding or extruding directly from or into the built forms in the same material gives a permanence as part of the physical makeup of the building. This also lends itself to a sense of environmental weightlessness. The invisibility of the sign material communicates the building's sustainable responsibility, avoiding the use of excessive materials and parts.

Playfulness and humanity
Given the function of this building, humor and humanity are important values in the design. Creating a juxtaposition to the relative formalism of the building by altering the expected axis within the material lends a degree of both organic and human quality to the way the typographic application unfolds. In a positive way it gives back emotion to a very functional facility. Van der Westhuyzen and Habicht hoped to create an identity and signage system less self-conscious in its relationship to the architecture.

Movement and exploration
Qualities of movement and temporal experimentation are also very much inherent in how the signage strategy could be extrapolated. As with the dynamic properties of the building's louver system, where articulated panels adjust to the position of the sun, the signage concept implied and created movement for different applications. To engage the public with a sense of movement, scale, and drama departs from the expected realm of what a sign does. For example, subtle angles of the type combined with symbols imply a direction. Intentional, minor disruption of the imbued order of the building brings back a lot of what communities hold closest to them: freedom and spirit. Van der Westhuyzen and Habicht planned for the signage to sit in an irregular manner and bring an element of natural disorder into the center. While still adhering to pragmatic needs, the signage prompts people through curiosity and engagement to make a unique connection with the building, the library, and the community center in their own interpretive way.

Typeface – Swiss
Material ± Production – Corian, wood, enamel
Architects – Collider Timenho Architects

CITY OF SYDNEY
SURRY HILLS LIBRARY
& COMMUNITY CENTRE
GROUND FLOOR
GROUND AND BASEMENT
LIBRARY

CITY OF SYDNEY
SURRY HILLS LIBRARY
& COMMUNITY CENTRE
LEVEL 1
LEVEL 2
CHILD CARE
VIA LIFT ONLY
LEVEL 1
SURRY HILLS
NEIGHBOURHOOD CENTRE
FUNCTION ROOM
GROUND AND BASEMENT
LIBRARY
VIA LIFT & STAIRS
TOILETS
LIFT

The function of a signage system—as in any other location—is to guide to the destiny one desires to go to, but education centers have specific needs that should be added to this basic function. Apart from guiding, can you inspire/motivate the learning process through a signage system?

While learning is about understanding existing knowledge, it is also about altering or improving established thinking. If signage systems can create a sense of difference and experimentation while doing their job, then they have the great ability to support the user's own learning experience associated with a physical place.

Signage for places of learning can arguably have a greater responsibility to its audience. Beyond an immediate function, it has the opportunity to create other stories with a greater sense of permanence, to speak to generations of users while having a thoughtfulness to leave a positive memory. This message outlives the practical function of the building/place itself and can even be a source of inspiration and motivation for students or patrons long after the fact. Signage that provides other levels of insight not only builds towards defining the personality of the place, but aids in the ownership and enjoyment of its users.

The nature of signage involves being highly sensitive to the needs of the user in a spatially pragmatic way. In some cases there are nuances and subtleties that inspire and elicit a wealth of secondary information, providing people with a lot more than the way to the bathroom.

*Andrew van der Westhuyzen
Clemens Habicht*

SCHOOL 03

by i29
Designer – i29
Client – Panta Rhei College

"Gossip about me, but don't tell them the truth. Make them believe something bigger."

Architecture and interior

In the design for the new accommodations of public school Panta Rhei in Amstelveen, Netherlands, there is a lot of attention to the balance between freedom and a sense of security. Snelder Architecten realized a building with many open multi-functional spaces where students can make themselves familiar with the teaching material. The interior design by i29 links up with that perfectly and gives the spaces an identity that connects with the students' environment and addresses them directly and personally. i29 let itself be inspired by the name of the school. Panta Rhei means "everything flows" or "everything is in motion." This led to a design that leaves space for the imagination of the users, offering elements that can be used flexibly, which also propagates the school's identity.

Poems

Throughout the entire school poems have been applied to the linoleum floors and the furniture. The thought behind this is that there are moments outside of the classroom when you can learn and gain insight: often a casual setting is very inspiring. Maybe these poems provide a different perspective in an unguarded moment. i29 commissioned the poet Erik Jan Harmens for this. He worked out themes like insecurity and friendship together with the students. The open texts leave room for their own interpretation. i29 modeled the poems in "carpets of text" in which the letters stick together and seem to flow from each other. From a distance the texts form intriguing graphic patterns. This imagery has been implemented by i29 in the new school logo, the facade, and the signposting throughout the school. The furniture, which was made to measure, is informal and dynamic. Because work takes place both in groups and individually, i29 itself designed tables in asymmetrical, angular shapes. These shapes allow the furniture to be linked together in all kinds of ways and different configurations can be made, such as square, circular, or star-shaped set-up. This means the pieces can be used in the general spaces as well as in the classrooms and staff rooms.

Structures

i29: "We think in structures and rhythms and not in taste or style. You can look at it as music which deals with harmony and contrast. One tone is not unconnected to the next and silence is essential." i29 has realized a spatial composition that has been carried out without compromise. Over the neutral basis of tables and benches there is a fine fabric of black elements consisting of the poems, the hassocks, and the Magis One-chairs. The furniture is strong and robust and does not look bulky, but rather refined. Remarkable in this context is the choice of the Grcic chair. It matches well here because of its technical aura and it urges you to think about the design and production process—this is a vocational school after all. Just because this is not a university, does not mean you do not have to challenge the students.

Field of tension

There is a field of tension between the free, blank character of the open spaces and the personal, almost emotional nature of the poems. Both have been carried to great lengths; in the sense that the spaces are very aloof and quiet, the text carpets speak to the children in a direct and personal way.

Typeface – by i29
Architects – Snelder Architects

TRAMELAN
CORPORATE IDENTITY AND VISUAL LANGUAGE

by onlab
Designer – onlab
Client – Municipality of Tramelan, Switzerland

Tramelan is a city situated in the Bernese Jura, the industrial region in Switzerland with a culture of watchmaking and engineering, where Nicolas Bourquin grew up. Tramelan had been shrinking for 25 years and in 2004 onlab was hired to take part in the commission examining the identity and development opportunities of Tramelan as advisors in the field of communication. The commission delivered a report analyzing the current (infra-)structural, political, economic, social, and cultural situation of the village and its local, regional, and national image, as well as its self-perception. Following this report, which was to be delivered to the foundation for extensive restructuring measures in 2006, onlab was commissioned to develop a new visual identity and communication strategy for the village for the years to come. In September 2007 the results of this project were presented to the population and to the press, with the new strategy being implemented successively. An exclusively designed typeface, *Tramelan-Lutz,* was derived from the typeface *Lutz* and reflected the typefaces originating in the industrial tradition, and the culture of watchmaking and engineering. The first visual identity of Tramelan was introduced in 1441 and is an adaption of the armorial bearings of the local duke. Over the centuries, different versions of the emblem with the three linden leafs emerged. In 1954, the council of Tramelan defined the emblem by nothing more than a sentence according to the heraldic tradition. This left a certain space for interpretations of the emblem. The new emblem is based on the new *Tramelan-Lutz* typeface. This solution gives a strong uniformity to the signage system. One additional element of the new visual identity is the diagonal, which is derived from the emblem. This basic element gives a strong identification value to the communication. The visual identity has been applied to different media, exhibitions, signage, etc. following the guidelines set up by onlab.

Typeface – Tramelan-Lutz (designed by onlab, based on Lutz)

CITY GARDEN HOTEL, ZUG

by Bringolf Irion Vögeli GmbH, Visuelle Gestaltung
Designer – Natalie Bringolf, David Bühler, Kristin Irion,
Judith Stutz
Client – MZ-Immobilien AG, Zug

Reflection is the central architectural theme of this four-star business hotel. The three-dimensional façade, with its serrated overhang, finds its counterpart in the sculpturally designed wings of rooms. The three-dimensional signage reflects the materiality and shapes of the building. In daylight the elements of the signage are perceived as sculptural objects; at night they are illuminated in a way that their surface can be seen from a distance.

Typeface – HTF Gotham
Material ± Production – Reflective coated numbers
Architects – EM2N Architekten, Zurich
Photographer – Bivgrafik

Photographer – Roger Frei, Zurich

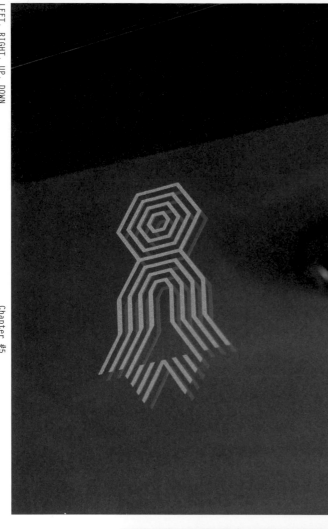

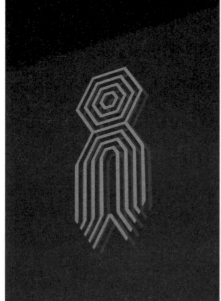

CIRCUS

by Mind Design
Designer – Mind Design
Client – Circus

Circus is a club and restaurant with a burlesque theme, featuring changing performances. Since the club interior features many mirrored surfaces, the design of the logo is based on the shape of a kaleidoscope. Other influences came from surrealism, art deco, *Alice in Wonderland*, animals, and the steps leading up to the large table that doubles as a stage. A main feature of the interior is a three-dimensional version of the logo built from different layers of perspex, set into a wall, and illuminated from the back in changing colors.

Typeface – Custom designed
Material ± Production – Layered sheets of acrylic, polished steel,
LED lights, etched mirror
Collaboration with Tom Dixon – Design Research Studio

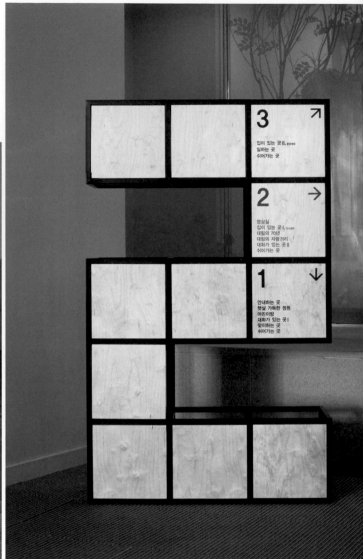

E-LIVING WORLD

by Workroom
Designer – Workroom
Client – Daelim Corporation

Signs hanging in a model home built by a Korean construction company. Floor directory signs on each floor were designed based upon a modularized rectangular room, which is the basis for many homes.

Typeface – Akzidenz Grotesk, SM Gothic Extra Bold
Material ± Production – Plywood, blackened steel plate, silkscreen
Photographer – Park Junghoon

ONE DAY POEM PAVILION
(EXPERIENTIAL TYPOGRAPHY)

by Jiyeon Song
Designer – Jiyeon Song
Client – Art Center College of Design

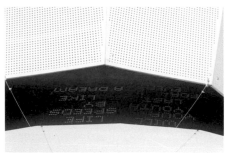

The results of an extensive exploration with shadows, the One Day Poem Pavilion demonstrates the poetic, transitory, site-sensitive, and time-based nature of light and shadow. Using a complex array of perforations, the pavilion's surface allows light to pass through creating shifting patterns, which—during specific times of the year—transform into the legible text of a poem. The specific arrangements of the perforations reveal different shadow-poems according to the solar calendar: a theme of new-life during the summer solstice, a reflection on the passing of time at the period of the winter solstice. The time-based nature of the poem—and the visitor's time-based encounters with it—allow viewers to have different experiences either seeing a stanza of the poem or getting the whole poem. All of these possible experiences are equally valuable and have meanings unique to the individual. This technique has the potential for producing particular effects and meanings within an architectural environment. Without the use of a source of power other than the sun, this project uses light and shadow to push the boundaries of communication and experiential delight.

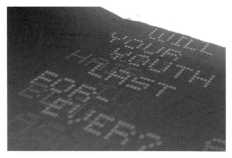

Typeface – Self-designed font by Jiyeon Song
Material ± Production – MDF, nuts and bolts
Media design program chair/lead thesis advisor – Anne Burdick
Thesis committee – Lisa Nugent, Tim Durfee, Peter Cho
Faculty advisors – Leah Hoffmitz, Lisa Krohn, Peter Lunenfeld, Phil van Allen, Martin Venezky, Norman Klein
Fabrication advisor – Wes Hanson (Art Center technical support center)

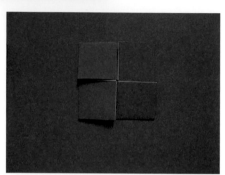

AFFICHAGE DIGITAL

by Etienne Cliquet
Designer – Etienne Cliquet
Client – NPAI

Exhibition commissionned by NPAI for
the Electroni[k] festival at the Galerie
Sortie des artistes and eight Galeries du
Théâtre in Rennes, France on October
16th and 17th, 2009 (24 hours non-stop).
By opening and closing paper-works
attached to the display "Affichage digital,"
one is able to picture various different
signs as letters or digits.

Material ± Production – Paper folding, paint

XIA-ZAI

by Etienne Cliquet
Designer – Etienne Cliquet

下仔 means in Chinese "to download" but also "to give birth" (xià zài in pinyin). It is a word game that is based upon a very similar pronunciation, valid for the written language (e-mail, msn, etc.). Apart from that, the icon for downloading is often a cow on the Chinese internet. "To download" represents for me an artistic contemporary gesture (despite the demonization of the subject by the law Hadopi 2). Nine of ten ideas in my work come more or less from preexisting ideas that I download from the web. The word game with the expression "to give birth" in Chinese reinforces the fertile character of the web and refers to to the French expression "accoucher d'une idée" (birth of an idea).

Material ± Production – Paper folding, black paint

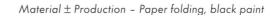

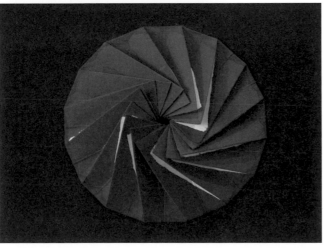

ALL-IN-ONE-NEWSPAPER

by Lesley Moore
Designer – Lesley Moore
Client – Tuttobene

For the 2007 presentation, Lesley Moore introduced the slogan "this is the way we see it" referring to sustainability as a selection criteria for the Tuttobene designers. Like the previous year, the entire presentation was designed with just one ingredient: the Tuttobene all-in-one newspaper. A handle-like cutout made it possible to hang the newspaper on the surrounding walls. A range of functions was created by reordering the pages of the newspaper in various ways, including signage, catalogue, flyer, plan, slogan, wallpaper, and individual posters for each designer.

Typeface – Helvetica, Times New Roman
Material ± Production – Rotation offset
Exhibition design in cooperation with Silke Spinner (www.silkespinner.com)
Photographer – Alberto Ferrero

RUS LIMA
¡SÚBETE AL TREN FANTASMA!
AUTOPARQUE PÚBLICO DE
DIVERSIONES
(GET ON THE GHOST TRAIN!
PUBLIC AUTO AMUSEMENT PARK)

by Basurama
Designer – Basurama and Lima artists (Christians Luna, Sandra Nakamura, Camila Bustamante, El Cartón, C.H.O.L.O., Play-stationvagon, El Codo, Los Colados and Motivando Corazones)

The project consisted in the transformation of the much controversial abandoned works of the elevated light railway of Lima, Perú into a self-constructed mini amusement park. Basurama and a series of Lima artists worked together with the community and, basically using trash and cheap materials, produced free-to-use amusements and reopened the platform for neighbors as an esplanade 25 years after it was built and abandoned. The goal was to show that public space can be created, enjoyed, and defended by the community by self-constructing it the same way they build their homes; apart from adding some color and fun to a grey and poor area of the city, they started a collective reflection about development, the need and desire for infra-structures, and creativity in general.

Photographer – Basurama

LETTERLAB

by Strange Attractors
Design – Ryan Pescatore Frisk + Catelijne van Middelkoop
Client – Graphic Design Museum, Breda, Netherlands

Letterlab is all about letters in the broadest sense of the word. In this exhibition, children (ages 6-13) and their parents discover that the letters you mostly encounter in books mean a great deal more.

Typeface – GDM Opa, GDM Bubbs, GDM Cowboy, GDM Second Hand Lenin, SAD 8, Porta

THE MAKING OF YOUR MAGAZINES
EXHIBITION

by onlab
Designer – onlab
**Client – Exhibition and project space by Arch+
as a contribution to Documenta 12 magazines**

The exhibition "The Making of Your Magazines" offers two
approaches to the 40 year history of *Arch+* discourse. The
mapping on the wall shows an overview and the development of
twelve themes. Folders at the desks offer a selection of articles of
five of the twelve themes for further reading. These articles are the
basis on which visitors can produce their own *Arch+* issue. Visitors
found folders with the selected articles right by the copy machine.
They would then staple their copies between two thicker sheets of
paper. The thicker paper came in two versions: a cover with an
Arch+ logo on it and a blank one for the backside. Visitors could
fold the exhibition poster into a cover for their magazine and
place the copies inside.

*Design, art direction – onlab Nicolas Bourquin, Sven Ehmann with
Murielle Badet, Cathy Larqué, Mélanie Schneider,
Maria Tackmann, Kasper Zwaaneveld*

UPDATING GERMANY
100 PROJECTS FOR A BETTER FUTURE

by onlab
Designer – onlab
**Client – Raumtaktik and Federal Ministry of Transport,
Building and Urban Affairs, Germany**

The German contribution to the 11th International Architecture
Exhibition at the Venice Biennale 2008 allegorizes the world is in
imbalance: economically, ecologically, and socially. 100 projects
are presented that claim sustainability and alternative energy; in
short, 100 projects for a better future.

*Art direction, exhibition design, graphic design – onlab, Nicolas
Bourquin, Murielle Badet, Anna Haas, Nathanaël Hamon, Linda
Hintz, Matthias Hübner, Gigi Ho, Rainalt Jossé, Renu Gautam,
Yvonne Schneider, Sueh Li Tan, Thibaud Tissot,
Judith Wimmer, Kasper Zwaaneveld
General commission – Raumtaktik, Friedrich von Borries,
Matthias Böttger
Communication – SBCA Sally Below Cultural Affairs*

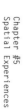

WORK FOR THE CBK, ROTTERDAM 2007

by Krijn de Koning
Designer – Krijn de Koning
Client – Sikkens Foundation + CBK

Temporary, site-specific work for the outside façade and interior of the Center for the Visual Arts (CBK), Rotterdam, 13.70 x 11.60 x 10.10 meters. Commissioned by the Sikkens Foundation and CBK Rotterdam. Initially, the commissioned work was for the façade of the building. Krijn de Koning proposed a work that was also for the inside of the building and that could be used by the organization. Besides being an emblematic object on the building, the work also had a strong and direct consequence for the way the artscenter would use their interior space.

Photographer – Ernst Moritz

WORK FOR Z33, HASSELT, 2009

by Krijn de Koning
Designer – Krijn de Koning
Client – Z33

Work for the entrance hall, Z33, Hasselt, Belgium. Temporary
artwork for the exhibition "Superstories" in Museum Z33, Hasselt,
Belgium, 2009.

GEWOON HARD KNALLEN

by StudioSpass VOF
Designer – StudioSpass, Jaron Korvinus & Daan Mens
Client – commissioned by TENT. Rotterdam

Gewoon Hard Knallen (Just Play Hard) is a provocative reference to the vision of one of Rotterdam's former leading design studios. While "hard work" was the designer's maxim in the 1980s, for this generation it is about making a noise. *Gewoon Hard Knallen* is an an-amorphous mural; it plays with the laws of perspective and is only fully visible and readable from one set position.

Typeface – Futura Extra Bold
Material ± Production – Paint, wood, carpet

50 X BEST VERZORGDE BOEKEN
(50 X BEST BOOK DESIGN)

by Lesley Moore
Designer – Lesley Moore
Client – Bijzondere Collecties + Stedelijk Museum Amsterdam

Graphic design for the exhibition "Best Dutch Book Design of 2008" in collaboration with EventArchitectuur.

Typeface – Universe
Exhibition design – EventArchitectuur (www.eventarchitectuur.nl)

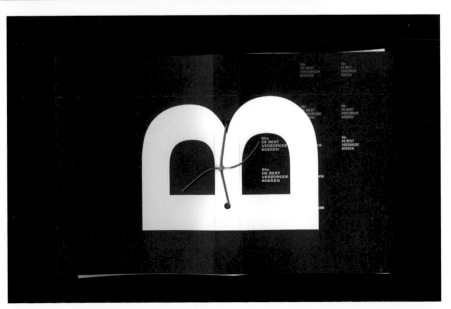

ABUNDANT AUSTRALIA
VENICE BIENNALE EXHIBITION IDENTITY

by Frost Design
Designer – Frost*
Client – Australian Institute of Architects (AIA)

A bright snapshot of architectural culture in Australia, the "Abundant" exhibition expresses the vigorous energy, exuberance, and diversity of our architectural past, present, and future. Vince Frost is one of five creative directors responsible for curating the Australian exhibition presented as part of the 11th International Architecture Exhibition, at the Venice Biennale in September 2008. Commissioned by RAIA, Frost Design also created the exhibition identity and logo. Vibrant yellow is strongly featured in the exhibition environment, as well as on print and marketing collateral, providing a sense of lively Australianess. The logo is inspired by the kaleidoscope of moving images featured in the upper gallery and delicately wavering garden of architectural models in the lower gallery. The multiple discs reference natural, structural, and experimental forms that inform Australia's hybrid architectural practice. The design responds to Venice Biennale director Aaron Betsky's theme: "Out there: architecture beyond building" and is rolled out across promotional brochures, postcards, invitations, and the exhibition catalogue.

Frost* Team
Creative director – Vince Frost
Design director – Quan Payne
Designers – Sarah Estens, Irmi Wachendorff
Junior designer – Francis Ratford
Architect – Joanna Mackenzie
Design management – Annabel Stevens
Creative directors of the Australian Pavilion at the 2008 Venice Architecture Biennale are architects Neil Durbach, Wendy Lewin and Kerstin Thompson, digital director Gary Warner, and design director Vince Frost

Bowl of clichés: In the northeast corner room, the flag turns into a giant abstract bowl and becomes virtual. It behaves like noodles in a soup and people can stir it. By doing this they find terms representing clichés. By touching them an explanation with pictures and text appears.

Interactive encyclopedia: On this part of the flag a keyboard is projected. Visitors can touch keys and get explanations of keywords dealing with the time of occupation of Austria.

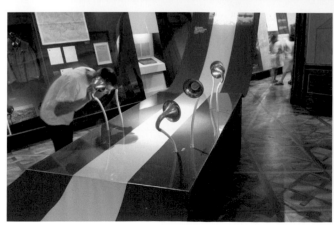

Ear-trumpet: The ear-trumpet allows visitors to listen into the flag to hear original recordings from politicians from the first decade of the last century, i.e., Emperor Franz Joseph I.

Flag camera: An old super8 camera was mounted on a slide and points into the flag. With this interface visitors can browse old private movies which are then projected onto the flag.

THE NEW AUSTRIA

by ART+COM AG
Designer – ART+COM
Client – Austrian Gallery of Belvedere

In 2005, Austria celebrated its 50th anniversary of the signing of the Austrian state treaty. For this occasion, an exhibition about Austria's history was shown in the Belvedere palace in Vienna. It consisted of three parts: on the left-hand wall objects, artifacts and documents explaining and contextualizing the Austrian history were exhibited. The right wall was furnished with important pieces of Austrian artwork. For the space in-between a 250 meters long winding Austrian flag was designed, passing through all exhibition rooms. The red and white ribbon interconnects history and art and guides the visitor's motion through the museum. The concept was to use the flag beyond that as a narrator to explain and comment on the national history. It acts as an interface for audiovisual media and provides several interactive installations. Thus content can be perceived with all senses along the flag trail, enabling visitors to actively participate in the exhibition. Different installation formats seamlessly come from the ribbon, always taking up the red white color scheme in their visual appearance.

Exhibition arrangement in cooperation with architect Martin Kohlbauer and Wolfgang Luser
Contents – Exhibition office Belvedere Gallery

Economy info sculpture: In this space the flag becomes a statistic sculpture representing the gross national product over the last century compared to the European GNP. Medial terminals indicate the reasons for peaks and declines.

EVENT STYLE EUROPEAN DESIGN FESTIVAL 2010

by Studio Dumbar
Designer – Studio Dumbar
Client – European Design Festival

Studio Dumbar was invited to develop the design of the 2010 festival, which was initiated in 2007 in Athens, and has since then traveled to Zurich, Stockholm and now Rotterdam. The festival's main objectives are:

- to celebrate European design with all its regional distinctive elements, as well as its common grounds
- to allow European designers to meet, benchmark, be inspired, and build networks
- to promote and raise standards for communication design throughout Europe
- to properly honor and award people who invest their passion in design

Studio Dumbar approached the design of this year's festival by raising questions to shift perspectives: design has become increasingly important in our current society, for business, government, and cultural life; it is not only about aesthetics, for the nice experience of beauty. It has a vital role, simply for society to communicate and function better. If that is the case, do we, in the current, global economic crisis, raise the right questions and address the current issues? Integrating the visual language of protest movements and abstractions of the European flags, design and debate, Studio Dumbar created a range of items such as banners, posters, t-shirts, flags, leaders, and set design that invite you to join the discussion.

Photographer – Pim Top

THEATERTREFFEN, BERLINER FESTSPIELE
(THEATER MEETING, BERLIN FESTIVAL)

by Kathrin Frosch
Designer – Kathrin Frosch
Client – Theatertreffen, Berliner Festspiele

Since 2003 designer Kathrin Frosch has developed the visual concept for the Theatertreffen, the most important german-speaking theater festival in Berlin. The "wimpel" is the main motive and three-dimensional festival signage; the small version presents the trophy. It is designed every year in a different context and spread through print, publications, merchandising, and temporary installation during the festival.

Typeface – Eurostyle
Photographer – Frederic Lezmi

Photographer – Kathrin Frosch

Photographer – Kathrin Frosch

Photographer – Frederic Lezmi

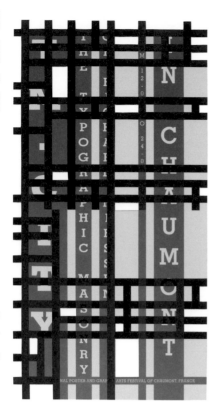

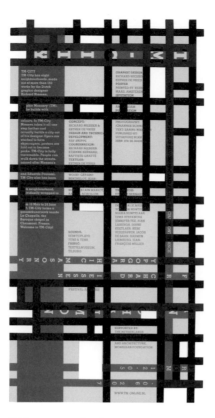

TM-City invitation; offset, die cut.

TM-City invitation; offset, die cut.

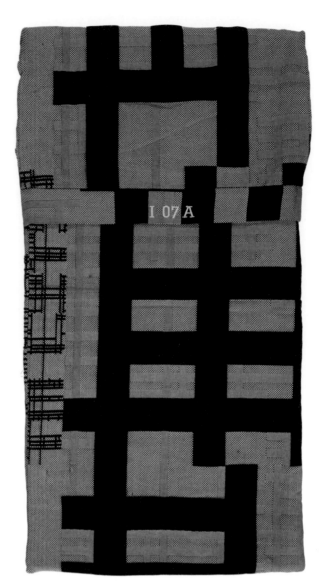

TM-City textile bag (one of 160 variations).

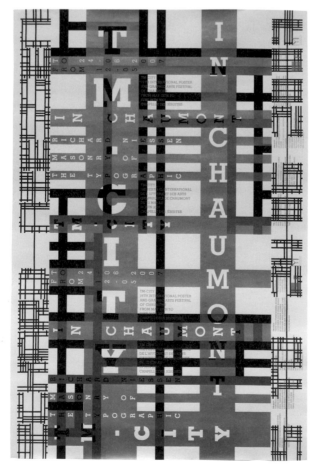

TM-City poster; silkscreen.

TM-CITY

by Niessen & de Vries
Designer – Niessen & de Vries
**Client – 18th International Poster and Graphic Arts Festival
of Chaumont, France**

Typeface – TM-City, Memphis

SKYLINE ZUIDOOST

by Niessen & de Vries
Designer – Niessen & de Vries with Jennifer Tee
Client – Stadsdeel Zuidoost

The abstracted and decorative forms inspired by the area create
a city skyline and play on the idea of architecture evolving to
become the type. The main inspiration for the creation of the
mural was traditional architecture from around the world. The
majority of the community in the area comes from African origins;
the fabrics and other graphic ephemera collected as research
in the neighborhood, employed unique patterns that helped to
create the design of the mural.

Material ± Production – Neon, silkscreen

DOCKING STATION

by Niessen & de Vries
Designer – Niessen & de Vries
Client – Stedelijk Museum

Docking Station was a special exhibition space in the (temporary) Stedelijk Museum CS near the harbor of Amsterdam; every six weeks the space exhibited a different up-and-coming artist. To reflect the dynamic and special status of this space within the museum, Niessen & de Vries decided to use the entrance of the exhibition area to visualize both what had been shown earlier, and what was still to come: a context for the individual exhibitions. They did so by devising a system inspired by industrial containers.

Typeface – Divers

Martin Del Amo

CHAPTER SIX
- SHIFTING LIGHTS -

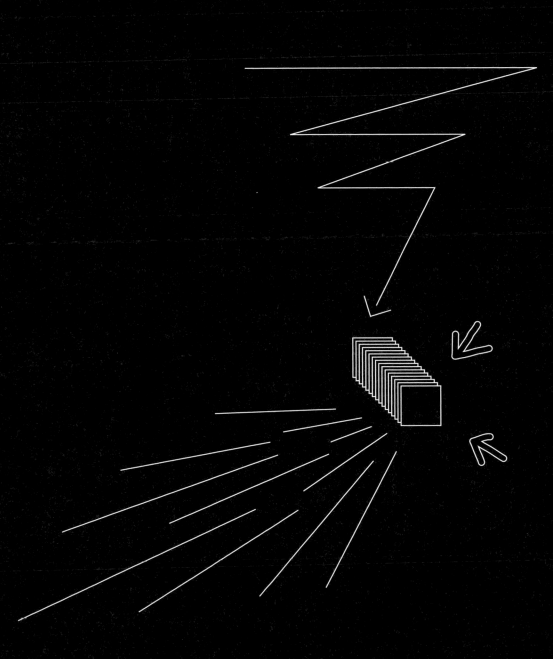

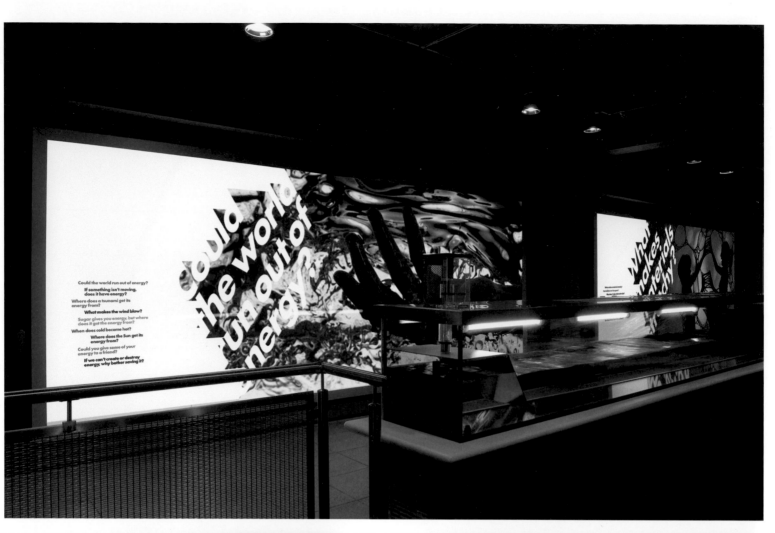

P#206

LAUNCHPAD

by Pentagram Design Limited
Designer – Harry Pearce
Client – The Science Museum, London

The Science Museum commissioned Harry Pearce at Pentagram to create the identity and exhibition graphics for a new and improved Launchpad gallery space within the popular London museum. The primary purpose of the redevelopment was to create a space that appeals to children between 8 and 14 and one that engages brains, not just fingers. The main logotype used is a very simple illusion; the perspective of the typography at the top is never resolved at the bottom, meaning the depth of the logo can be extended indefinitely. This extendable shadow can thus be used to contain virtually anything: a color, a texture, an image, a piece of film. The identity has been used throughout the gallery to create a series of graphic devices that can be applied to walls and back-lit displays.

Partner/designer – Harry Pearce
Designer – Richard Wilson

P#209

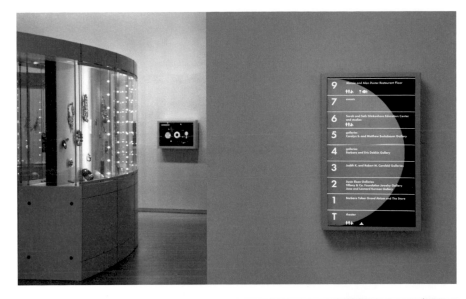

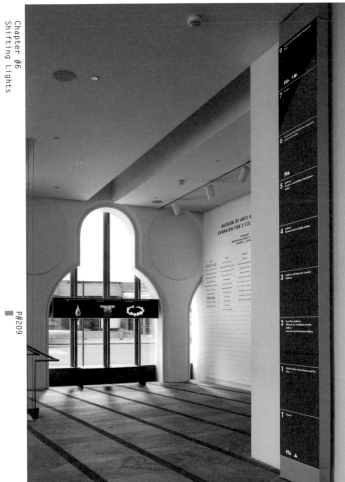

MUSEUM OF ARTS AND DESIGN

by Pentagram Design Limited
Designer – Lisa Strausfeld
Client – Museum of Arts and Design

Pentagram created a new identity and a program of signage
and dynamic digital media for the Museum of Arts and Design
to coincide with the opening of the institution's new home at the
refurbished 2 Columbus Circle in New York. The program of
signage and dynamic digital media includes animated totems
that serve as directories to the various floors of the museum,
ground-floor screens facing the sidewalks that let passers-by know
what is happening inside, and interpretive kiosks with interactive
databases that let visitors explore the collection. Pattern is a
major element of the identity, as it is for the museum's art, and the
interactive media installations present a shifting pattern of objects
from the collection.

Creative director – Lisa Strausfeld
Designers – Lisa Strausfeld, Christian Marc Schmidt,
Christian Swinehart

RUHR MUSEUM ESSEN

by L2M3 Kommunikationsdesign GmbH
Designer — David Arzt, Frank Geiger, Sascha Lobe
Client – Stiftung Ruhr Museum, Essen

One part of the Zollverein Coal Mine World Cultural Heritage Site is the former coal wash plant converted by Rem Koolhaas, which has housed the Ruhr Museum since January 2010. Visitors experience a succession of very different impressions and discover an equally checkered history. The visual identity in the form of DNA code is constituted by a typographical system that imprints itself in different aggregate states into the exhibition. Based on the idea of a mine car or container, the individual words sit more or less exactly in a grid system of areas. This gives rise to a rhythm that appears mechanical and which is formulated in the form of graphics and objects.

Typeface – FF DIN
Architects - O.M.A. Stedebouw B.V., Office for Metropolitan Architecture, Rotterdam
Heinrich Böll Architekt BDA DWB, Essen
Exhibition design - HG Merz Architekten Museumsgestalter

4TH INTERNATIONAL ARCHITECTURE BIENNALE ROTTERDAM, OPEN CITY: DESIGNING COEXISTENCE

by Mevis & van Deursen
Designer – Mevis & Van Deursen
Client – 4th International Architecture Biennale Rotterdam

The starting point for the signage of the exhibition "Open City" was to look into existing ways of communication within our public space. Different messages need different forms, thus for this exhibition Mevis & van Deursen used three different methods (carriers) for adding information: light on the ceiling, paper on the walls, and objects on the tables. They created a set of rules for each method and worked with the students of the Werkplaats Typografie, Netherlands, for the execution of each of them.

Typeface – Neon Typeface by Karl Nawrot
Thanks to the students of Werkplaats Typografie, Netherlands
Photographer – Michelle Wilderom

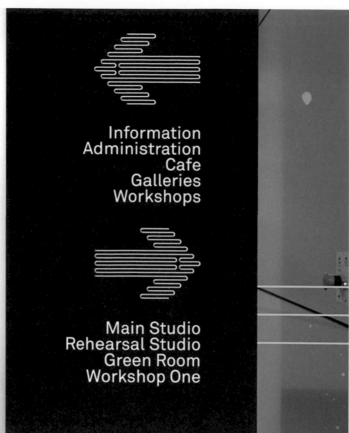

Information
Administration
Cafe
Galleries
Workshops

Main Studio
Rehearsal Studio
Green Room
Workshop One

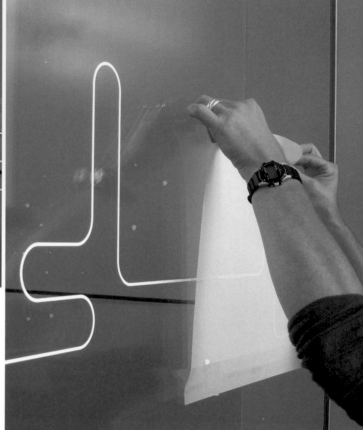

CAMPBELLTOWN ARTS CENTER

by Sam Frith
Designer – Sam Frith
Client – Campbelltown Arts Center

This new art center had no wayfinding signage in place. They wanted an interim solution to guide visitors from the main entrance to reception, while informing them of what events were on at the time. Sam Frith could not think of a clearer way of directing people than with a gigantic neon arrow. Incorporated into this was a flat screen LCD that communicates up-to-date exhibition and activity info. The graphic language of the arrow's form was extended to develop a series of lines and typography that could be used for other communications and collateral, creating an almost macro-identity for the center.

Typeface – Custom typeface
Project management – Ian Wingrove

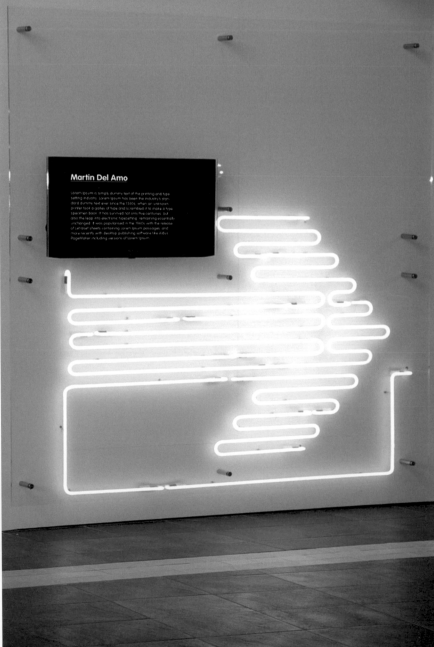

Martin Del Amo

LA CINÉMATHÈQUE FRANÇAISE, PARIS, FRANCE

by Integral Ruedi Baur Paris, Zurich, Berlin
Designer – Integral Ruedi Baur Paris, Zurich, Berlin
**Client – Sponsors: Ministère de la Culture et de la Communication, l'Émoc and
the Cinémathèque française**

Orientation and visual identification system, external and internal signage, and lighting system for the façade (1% artistique).

*Project developed by Irb Paris Team – Ruedi Baur, Stéphanie Brabant, Olivier Duzelier, Toan Vu-Huu
Collaborators – Thomas Hundt of Jangled Nerves (Audiovisual design), Vadim Bernard (Visual animations)
Architect for the building renovation – Dominique Brard of l'Atelier de l'Île
Photographer – Stéphane Dabrowski, Graziella Antonini*

Brühltor-Passage

Bahnhof
Stiftsbezirk Unesco Welterbe
Stiftsbibliothek
Kathedrale
Altstadt
Marktplatz
Kantonsschulpark
Parkhaus Burggraben
Parkhaus Brühltor

Brühltor-Passage

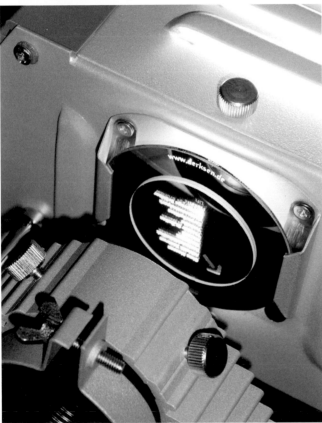

P#219

BRÜHLTOR PASSAGE, ST. GALLEN
SIGNAGE DESIGN

by Inform
Designer – Felix Hartmann
Client – City of St. Gallen, Switzerland

Brühltor was once a city gate. The Brühltor underpass is still an important access to the old town; it combines the old with the museum quarter and it is the western entrance to the enlarged and redesigned 2006 City Parking Brühltor, which had been planned since 1999. In the fall of 2007 the construction began. The architects simplified the layout geometry, cleared obstacles from the path, widened the passage from the city parking, and regulated the shop fronts, thus the improved perspective, which now brings more focus. The lighting concept, materials, and colors combine in a friendly atmosphere that enhances the sense of security. The solution lays in the use of so-called "gobos," which means "graphical optical black out." Gobos are actually slide-projectors—they project still images or writings on a glass slide to the floor. Inform determined the points at which there are several ways to select and therefore require information on the objectives in the outside world. They mounted a gobo on each of these points that now function day and night, depending on which light concept its messages project to the ground.

Typeface – Univers
(according to the corporate identity of City St. Gallen)
Material ± Production – Gobo projectors
(graphical optical black out)

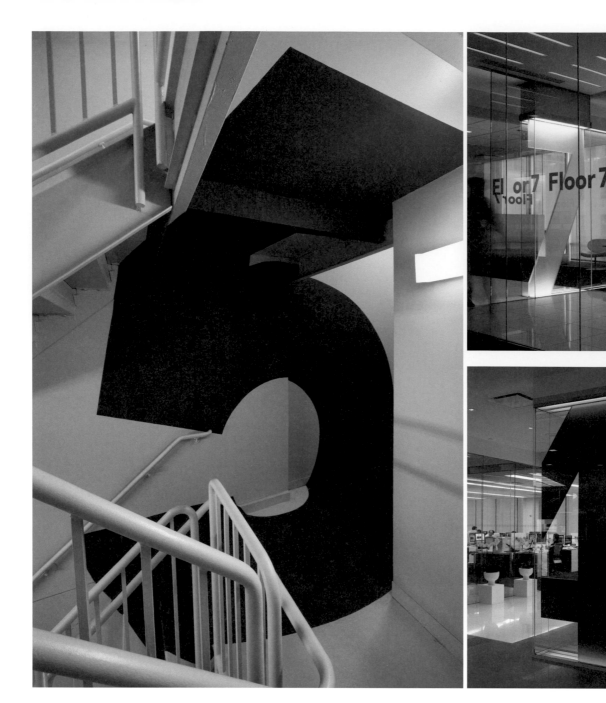

BLOOMBERG L.P. CORPORATE HEADQUARTERS
ENVIRONMENTAL GRAPHICS

by Pentagram Design Limited
Designer – Paula Scher
Client – Bloomberg L.P.

Pentagram created the signage, environmental graphics, and media installations for the corporate headquarters of Bloomberg, the financial news, data, and analytics provider. The company occupies nine floors as the anchor tenant of a new 55-story mixed-use tower at 731 Lexington Avenue on Manhattan's East Side. Working with STUDIOS Architecture, Pentagram created an interior that seamlessly communicates Bloomberg's product brand and services—data, news, and information—to employees, clients, and visitors. This environment of numbers includes identification signage for floors, rooms, and elevators; directory signage and wayfinding; and several dynamic, superscale media installations, which display live content from Bloomberg's own news and data feeds. Pentagram also created a digital media distribution system for easy content management of the information displays.

Art directors – Paula Scher (Environmental Graphics),
Lisa Strausfeld (Dynamic Media)
Designers – Paula Scher, Lisa Strausfeld, Rion Byrd, Jiae Kim, Andrew Freeman

Dynamic Media for Bloomberg Corporate Headquarters

METEOCOLONNADE
DYNAMIC INFORMATION SCULPTURE

by ART+COM AG
Designer – ART+COM
Client – Port Bregenz

Widely visible by day and at night, the four LED columns inform skippers and visitors of the harbor Bregenz about Lake Constance's current conditions: water level, water temperature, air temperature, and wind speed and direction. This data must be shown at the harbors for security reasons but is commonly written on blackboards or standard screens. When rebuilding the complete port area, the regional government decided to look for a more sophisticated level display coming up to the new information center's clear-lined architecture. Inside the undulated center, the three meters high LED pillars present the measurement results transferred every five minutes from different lake stations and processed in real time. ART+COM designed each column with individual personality, reflecting the information it is communicating. The water level column, for example, ripples like the lake's surface. In addition to the real time data, the installation occasionally presents historical information to provide context to the current readings. Short animations show the record flood marks, the development of water quality, and annual averages. The luminous information is shown on both sides and provides a good legibility even over a great distance. At night its long-distance signal effect reaches even further, forming a reference point for the whole harbor area.

Material ± Production – LED-steles with 1cm pixel pitch

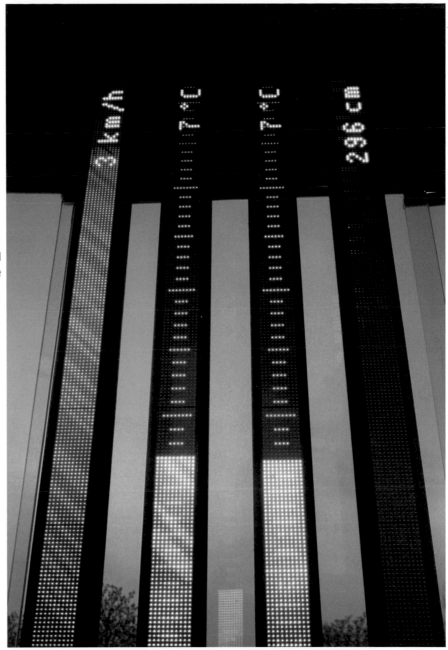

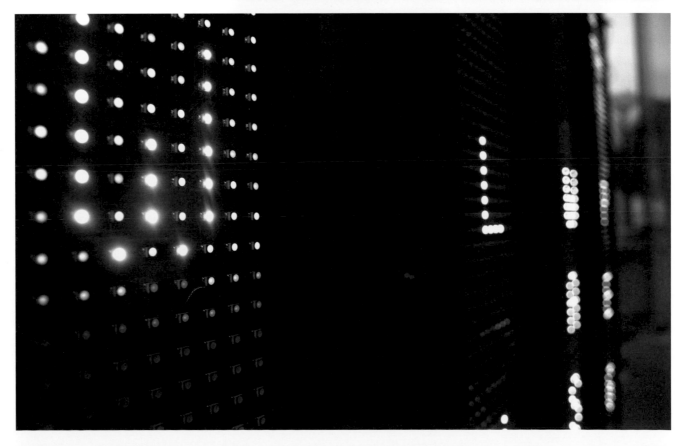

FROM	AIRPORT CODE	DATE		AIRPORT NAME		DATE	
	THX			THE HAGUE INT'L			
TO	RUNWAY LENGTH	TIME		RUNWAY ELEVATION		TIME	
	415 METERS			0.8 METERS			

FROM	CITY	DATE		COUNTRY		DATE	
	THE HAGUE			NETHERLANDS			
TO	COUNTRY ABBREVIATION		WORLD AREA CODE			TIME	
	NL			461			

FROM	LONGITUDE	DATE		LATITUDE		DATE	
	4° 18' 43.39"			52° 04' 35.51"			
TO	GMT OFFSET	TIME		TERMINALS		TIME	
	+1.0			1			

FROM	DESTINATIONS	DATE		FROM		DATE	
	20						
TO	FLIGHTS	TIME		TO		TIME	
	200						

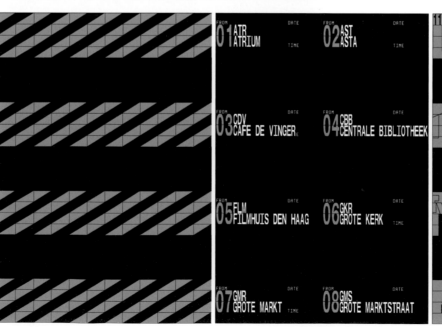

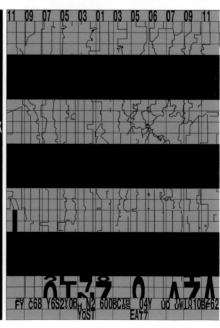

THX, THE HAGUE INT'L

by LUST
Designer – LUST
Client – TodaysArt

Turning the city of The Hague into
an International Airport. The Grote
Marktstraat—600 meters long—was
transformed into a landing strip, using
36 x 6 individual controllable lights and
48 x 2000 watt speakers, creating the
experience of airplanes landing in the
street. The landing strip connected the
two main areas of the festival with a total
of more than 25 stages throughout the
city. The Volharding building functioned
as an arrivals and departures sign, all
tied together by audio announcements
of incoming artists in eight different
languages.

*Typeface – Helvetica
Concept and design of landing strip – LUST
Soundscape, light control,
programming of landing strip – Mike Rijnierse,
Detlef Villerius, Basten Stokhuizen Concept,
design and programming of Volharding
building – LUST*

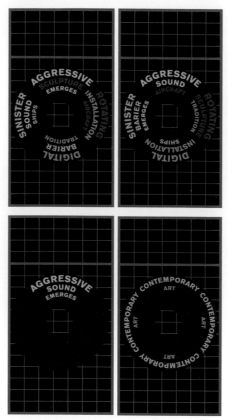

PROPOSAL FOR TRUCK LIFT SIGNAGE

by LUST
Designer – LUST
Client – Stedelijk Museum Amsterdam

The concept for the Stedelijk Museum identity revolved around ideas of scale (in time, in place, in content) and the development of a meta-language. Any kind of information all around the museum is set in a specific circular grid. The grid consists of five rings with different width. From the inside to the outside the rings become wider and thicker. The placed text adjusts in size to the scale of the rings. The various scaled text-sizes visualize the concept. The illustrations show proposals; LED signage systems for the trucklift, neon for the museum cafe, signage for the lift, and a mobile sign in the city of Amsterdam.

Typeface – Akzidenz Grotesk

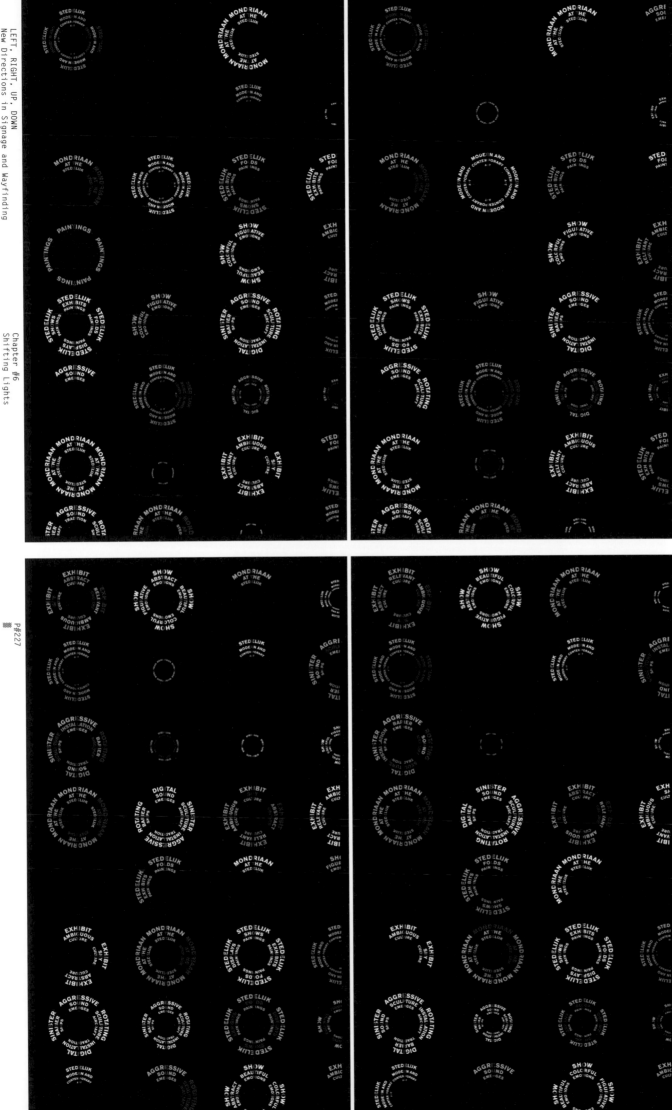

DRIVE BY

by Electroland LLC
Designer – Electroland LLC
Client – J.H. Snyder Co.

A custom 73 meters long electronic display alternates between
two modes: alphanumeric letters spell out famous lines from
Hollywood films; abstract letterforms follow cars as they pass by
and display collisions as cars pass each other.

Material ± Production – LED lights, video tracking, computer
Principal – Cameron McNall
Partner – Damon Seeley
Software developer – Eitan Medelowitz
Software architecture – Bradley Geilfuss
Act One Communications Inc.

CONNECTION

by Electroland LLC
Designer – Electroland LLC
Client – Indianapolis Airport

The pedestrian bridge connecting the parking garage with the new airport terminal is the main path into the airport for the majority of visitors and therefore serves as the gateway and introduction to the airport. Forty-six linear meters of the ceiling of the pedestrian bridge is covered with a field of interactive illuminated dots. These dots display several colors and exhibit a range of intelligent and playful behaviors. The dots can light up exactly over where the visitors stand and are able to fix on and follow a visitor down the length of the walk. Most importantly, they can connect several passengers to each other—hence the multiple meanings of "connection." The overhead dots call out the shifting relationships of movement generated by the visitors. The project also features sounds that reinforce the patterns occurring overhead.

Material ± Production - LED lights, stereo video tracking,
sound, computers
Principal - Cameron McNall
Partner - Damon Seeley
Software developer - Aaron Siegal
Software architecture - Bradley Geilfuss
Hale Microsystems LLC

PULSE

by Electroland LLC
Designer – Electroland LLC
Client – Los Angeles Fashion Center

A 40 meters long LED display pulses with blue light patterns,
activated by passing cars. Tracking is accomplished with a video
camera mounted on the roof.

Material ± Production – LED lights, video tracking, aluminum rails,
plexiglass diffuser, computer
Principal – Cameron McNall
Partner – Damon Seeley
Programmers – Aaron Siegal, Bradley Geilfuss
Manager – Matt Au

QUARTIER DES SPECTACLES, MONTREAL

by Integral Ruedi Baur Paris, Zurich, Berlin
Designer – Integral Ruedi Baur Paris, Zurich, Berlin
Client – Sponsor: Quartier des spectacles Partnership

Project carried out following an urban design competition won in 2005 in collaboration with Intégral Jean Beaudoin, architect, Montreal.

Project developed by Irb Paris, Irb Zurich, and Ijb Montreal Team – Ruedi Baur, Jean Beaudoin, Axel Steinberger, Antje Kolm, Simon Burkart, Charles Gignoux, Nicolas Schuybroek, Amélie Bilodeau, David Hopkins, Bruno Cloutier, Bryan Lamonde, Samuel Buteau, Ming Cheng Fu, Anne Passerieux

LOS ANGELES AUTHOR WALL

by Electroland LLC
Designer – Electroland LLC
Client – Los Angeles Department of Cultural Affairs

Electroland created a touchscreen interactive experience where visitors could navigate through and find information about hundreds of writers who have been associated with Los Angeles. All of the interactions were displayed on a huge projection as part of the Los Angeles contribution to the Guadalajara Book Fair.

Material ± Production – Touchscreen, video projectors, computer
Principal – Cameron McNall
Partner – Damon Seeley
Collaborator – Andy Goldman
Architects – John Friedman, Alice Kimm
Software developer – Aaron Siegal
Software architecture – Bradley Geilfuss

THE FIRST SEAL – IT WOULD BE BETTER IF YOU HAVE NEVER BEEN BORN...

by TSANG Kin-Wah
Designer – TSANG Kin-Wah

"The Seven Seals" is an ongoing series of seven digital video installations using texts and computer technology to show Tsang's thoughts on various issues of the day. "The Seven Seals" draws its reference from various sources including the Bible, Judeo-Christian eschatology, existentialism, metaphysics, politics, etc., which all attempt to articulate the complex situation of the world and the dilemmas that people are facing while approaching the end of the world. Animated phases and short sentences appear, move, and float, sometimes like a murmur and sometimes like an admonition that reveals the nature of human beings and the changes of our emotions. The texts remind us of issues like war, terrorism, revolution, death, murder, suicide, self-denial, etc. Without a clear beginning or end, each installation in the "The Seven Seals" creates different cycles of text on continuous loops that appear to repeat without end; echoing the concept of "eternal recurrence" whereby all the issues and dilemmas of daily existence are seen perpetually recurring for an infinite number of fleeting instances, even though we recognize and are aware of them for a much longer time.

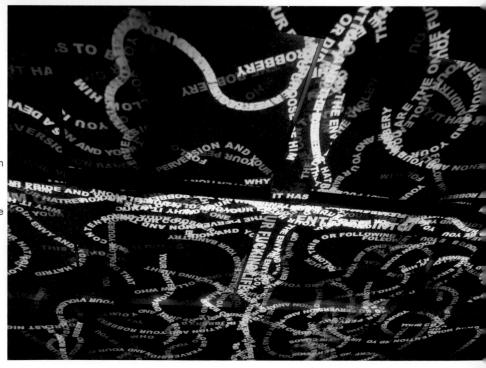

Typeface – Arial Black
Material ± Production – Computers, projectors, speakers

THE SECOND SEAL – EVERY BEING THAT OPPOSES PROGRESS SHOULD BE FOOD FOR YOU

by **TSANG Kin-Wah**
Designer – TSANG Kin-Wah

LEFT, RIGHT, UP, DOWN

NEW DIRECTIONS IN SIGNAGE AND WAYFINDING

Edited by TwoPoints.Net
Interview with Paula Scher by Martin Lorenz
English translation of Vier5 text by Simon Sinclair

Design by TwoPoints.Net
Typeface: Futura
Project management by Julian Sorge for Gestalten
Production management by Vinzenz Geppert for Gestalten
Proofreading by Rebecca Silus
Printed by Artes Graficas Palermo, S.L., Madrid
Made in Europe

Published by Gestalten, Berlin 2010
ISBN 978-3-89955-312-3

For more information, please visit www.gestalten.com

Bibliographic information published by the Deutsche Nationalbibliothek. The Deutsche Nationalbibliothek lists this publication in the Deutsche Nationalbibliografie; detailed bibliographic data is available online at http://dnb.d-nb.de.

None of the content in this book was published in exchange for payment by commercial parties or designers; the inclusion of all work is based solely on its artistic merit.

This book has been printed according to the internationally accepted ISO 14001 standards for environmental protection, which specify requirements for an environmental management system.

This book has been printed on FSC certified paper, which ensures responsible paper sources. FSC is a non-profit organization that promotes environmentally appropriate, socially beneficial, and economically viable management of the world's forests.

Gestalten is a climate-neutral company and so are our products. We collaborate with the non-profit carbon offset provider myclimate (www.myclimate.org) to neutralize the company's carbon footprint produced through our worldwide business activities by investing in projects that reduce CO_2 emissions (www.gestalten.com/myclimate).

* The TwoPoints.Net team that worked on this book:
Martin Lorenz, Lupi Asensio, David Nagel, Kosmas Sidiropoulos, Felix Auer, and Raby-Florence Fofana.